Descended

Descended

Searching for My Gullah-Geechee Roots

KEITH RUSHING

Published by the University of South Carolina Press
Columbia, South Carolina 29208

uscpress.com

Printed in the United States of America

Library of Congress Cataloging-in-Publication Data
can be found at http://catalog.loc.gov/.

ISBN: 978-1-64336-562-6 (hardcover)
ISBN: 978-1-64336-563-3 (ebook)

To my maternal ancestors,
Shirley Ruth "Adeyemi" Rushing,
Margaret Ruth Pearson, Sarah Christopher Polite,
Sancho Christopher, Prince Christopher,
Heena Christopher, Margaret "Molly" Jenkins,
and Benis Jenkins

There are stories and lives to liberate—stories and lives that can liberate us. All of us.

—TRACY K. SMITH

CONTENTS

LIST OF ILLUSTRATIONS

PREFACE

The Name That Launched a Journey

Soon after ABC first aired the TV series *Roots*, my seventh-grade teacher asked us to pursue our own mini-roots projects. We had to ask our oldest living relatives about the oldest ancestors they could remember. The story of Alex Haley's family tracing back to an African ancestor named Kunta Kinte, who came to America from The Gambia, had sparked tremendous interest in origin stories among Black people. Although the book later largely proved fictional, for African Americans it ignited conversations about slavery and particularly the origins of ancestors who were captured and bound for the United States aboard ships carrying the enslaved.

Aunt Aggie (short for Agnes) seemed like the perfect fit for my assignment. At the time, she was 80 years old. Born in 1897, she was the oldest of my grandmother's five siblings who were all born on the family farm in Hilton Head Island, South Carolina. My parents invited Aunt Aggie, who lived not far away in Jamaica, Queens, over to our house in Springfield Gardens (also in Queens) to spend the night. As we sat mostly in silence around the kitchen table, she racked her brain, digging up names long buried in her memory. My mother would add them to the family tree spread out in front of her. Aggie remembered many cousins and the surnames of people who married into the family. Mom remembered names she had heard and people she may have met who lived in the South, not New York City, where we lived. Aunt Aggie could go back as far as her grandparents, Sancho (pronounced "Sankoh") and Margaret "Molly" Christopher. I later learned they were born into bondage on a cotton plantation in Hilton Head in the 1840s. After Sancho served in the Civil War among the US Colored Troops, they transitioned to life as freedpeople. That knowledge would surface decades later, however, after archival documents revealed details of Sancho's life during and after the war.

Aunt Aggie and my father, Lawrence, in the living room of our home in Queens, NY. This picture was taken around the time she told us the name of Sancho Christopher in 1977.

Back in 1977, the name Sancho fired up my imagination. I wondered if Sancho would be the Kunta Kinte in my family. Could he be the ancestor who survived the excruciating journey to America aboard a slave ship? And where was he from? When I asked Aunt Aggie if Sancho, which she pronounced more like Sanku, was an African name, she said she didn't know. But I thought I was on to something. And I was. I wasn't aware of any Black folks at the time who had African names in their ancestral lineage. And I've met very few since.

This first glimpse of African heritage in my family stretches back some 200 years. I would learn that Sancho was indeed an African name. It was also among thousands of African names that were part of the Gullah-Geechee naming tradition. The Gullah-Geechee, for those unaware, are a group of African Americans who have lived in the coastal areas of North Carolina, South Carolina, Georgia, and Florida since the era of enslavement. They have maintained closer connections to the African cultures they descended from than African Americans in other regions of the country. The Gullah-Geechee culture was the culture that Aunt Aggie and my grandparents were born into but didn't discuss. Nobody acknowledged that our heritage was somehow unique or different from the heritages of other African Americans.

But at family gatherings, Gullah-Geechee culture showed up at the table in dishes like Cousin Kitty's red rice and Uncle Green's sweet potato pone, called tata pone. Once, when I told my grandmother I didn't like okra, she whipped up some okra gumbo, another dish with Gullah-Geechee origins—and told me that lightly frying it in thin slices to reduce the sliminess, would get me to like it. And she was right. Then there was the time Grandma took a trip back to Hilton Head Island to see some of the oldest people on the island. Afterward, she told me something in the Gullah-Geechee Creole and explained it to me. The Gullah-Geechee culture was ever present, understood like a family secret you know but don't talk about.

The name Sancho was the initial clue, the first glimpse of this unique heritage that would lead me on a journey to this more African past and my family's role in the Civil War when my ancestors took up arms to liberate themselves. Research about Sancho would take me back to the only town established by the federal government during the Civil War that was built by Black people and run by Black people. I would learn about how Black people chose to live as landowners and subsistence farmers on an almost all-Black island of Gullah-Geechee people with concepts of land and spirituality molded by their African heritage.

In the research for this book, I sought to fill a void, a void that many African Americans feel: a longing, a missing sense of connectedness to the past. I, like most Black people, did not choose this void but have been forced to live within its space. We know so little about our past, our ancestors' stories, their history and sometimes diffused and unrecognizable aspects of our heritage. Many, especially those of us who live in the North and are descendants of the Great Migration, know little beyond what our parents and grandparents chose to share about their lives and maybe a story or two about those who lived before their parents. Often, we know nothing beyond the town or city where they lived. And although African Americans' lineage in the United States—for those who are the descendants of the enslaved—extends well into the 1600s and 1700s, we don't know the names of ancestors who lived in bondage nor what their lives were like after enslavement. We are left to gather whatever we can from history books. The truth of their lives, the struggles of endurance and resistance, achievements, and hardships are unavailable to us; their legacies, cultural values, and heritage all but erased.

Our connection to Africa, where most of our ancestors originated, is even more deeply shrouded in mystery. We don't know what villages, cities, or kingdoms they came from. Nor do we know their ethnicities or what languages they spoke. The institution of slavery destroyed our ancestors' familial ties and their ability to communicate in Indigenous African languages and hindered their ability to maintain cultural values, ideas, practices and concepts, and familial and societal structures.

For many African Americans, the need to connect to our ancestral origins, our history, our family stories and cultures is essential to fully understanding our identity. Knowing aspects of our cultural heritage—what was lost, what was erased, and what was maintained—would help fill the void before the trauma and dispossession of slavery ripped it from us. Knowing this history, the familial and ancestral stories, might connect us to a place and space where we feel more whole, our feet planted firmly on solid ground—perhaps providing some solace and protection from the dehumanization, rejection, and alienation we live with every day.

Delving into the past also requires opening our consciousness to pain and trauma, the things over which we had no control, but still are connected to who we are today. However, when we research our family origins and uncover truths of what African Americans including our individual families achieved, it can fill the historical record in a deeply personal way while also combating erasure. Additionally, the journey into the past is a spiritual one, existential and transcendent, more fully linking us to the African diaspora, which we are surely part of. The journey requires that we learn history that our parents, grandparents, and ancestors failed to pass on, or refused to, perhaps out of pain or shame or the seeming irrelevance to the present.

I am by no means alone as a Black writer or artist in embarking on such a journey digging into my Southern roots and ancestral past. Writer Morgan Jerkins wrote about the "sense of loss" she carried well into adulthood. "I knew what it was like to carry blank spaces and missing pieces. We had no confidence in our origins as African Americans," she wrote in her book published in 2020. What was missing impacted how she felt about her identity. "My body, like my lineage, was a mystery. Because I didn't have a full narrative from either of my two families, I was not confident in my identity and culture."[1]

For Jerkins, who, like me, is a descendant of the Great Migration, the disconnect is perhaps greater when you haven't spent time in the physical spaces where your ancestors lived and don't know Southern relatives well. Jerkins went to various regions of the South, including the South Carolina Lowcountry to learn more. "The only way to find out was to make a journey in reverse and create symbolic bridges between those families who fled and those who remained on the lands of their people."[2]

Jon-Sesrie Goff, who grew up in New York and Connecticut, produced a 2023 documentary *After Sherman* that aired on PBS and focused on his journey to connect to his Gullah-Geechee roots near Charleston in Georgetown, South Carolina. Georgetown was a center of rice plantations during enslavement and a place where Gullah-Geechee families lived and owned land when they became freedpeople. In the film, Goff tells how his father, Reverend Norvell Goff (who was born there) would always tell him that he had both a birthplace and a home place. And his home place was in Georgetown. His father tells him of their ancestral connection to water. "The people here came by water. They lived by the water. And eat from the water. We are water people," he tells him.[3] After going South, Goff feels more certain that his father is right. "I'm Gullah," he said in the film. "Born in exile." The connection to land and a large extended family in Georgetown grounds him. When he talks of Georgetown, he says: "Where else do we have land, where else do we own homes, where else do we have a nucleus of families and cousins that come back on a consistent basis."

Along with Jerkins and Goff, I believe that the Great Migration which drove millions from the South was a forced migration that disrupted rootedness. Jerkins said: "Movement was as much an individual dream as a collective means of survival. We had to move to save our families, move to get better jobs and earn money, or move because we had this unwavering belief, despite endless oppression, that there was a different kind of beauty to be found in another zip code."[4]

Goff discussed the impact of the migration, explaining that families were first broken up during the transatlantic slave trade, then again broken up by enslavers during slavery and, yet again, broken up by the Great Migration. "Think of how many people left the South and went up North. They know they have people down here, but they don't know who those people are."

The Great Migration in my family came with not only physical distance but some cultural distancing among my relatives. What has played out across a couple of generations resembles themes of Julie Dash's groundbreaking 1991 film *Daughters of the Dust*, which spread awareness of the Gullah-Geechee culture more broadly.[5] *Daughters of the Dust* was riven with the tension within a Gullah-Geechee family around leaving the Sea Islands for better economic opportunities and staying in the land of their ancestors. Nana Peazant, the family matriarch, holds fast to her cultural ways and strives to keep the family connected while worrying about the loss of family bonds for her adult children and grandchildren who plan to leave. Those moving to the mainland also seek to distance themselves from the culture of the Sea Islands. Most saw Nana Peazant's amulets, derived from West African belief systems, and her faith that the ancestors are watching over the living, as old-fashioned and backward.

While I didn't hear pejorative views about Gullah-Geechee culture, my grandmother returned to Hilton Head only once as an elder, many decades after she left. I think my great-grandmother might have gone back once for a funeral. And one of my grandmother's older sisters, Mabel, also seldom returned. While the cuisine showed up, the Gullah-Geechee Creole wasn't spoken or discussed with the exception of my Uncle (Wilson) Green, Mabel's husband. And I didn't hear much discussion about Hilton Head except for the stories my grandmother shared. Perhaps most important is the physical and emotional disconnection that happened from moving North. A couple generations that were born and raised in New York have never visited Hilton Head and don't know the relatives who live there. And some level of silence about the past came with a loss of family history, cultural connection, ancestral heritage, and place.

But Goff notes that Black people are trying to learn and deepen their knowledge of their ancestral lands and the family members left behind. "People are trying to figure out where their roots are, who they're connected to—not just trying to find out what their African DNA is . . . People are really trying to connect back to people that are literally their people. Being here on this land has allowed me to come back and connect with my people that are here," he said.[6]

Poet Tracy K. Smith delves into her ancestral past to get a deeper sense of how they survived and endured. Raised in Connecticut, she returned to Sunflower, Alabama, to learn more about her paternal lineage. Smith talks about having to conduct the research amid the silence of family members and the erasure of a power structure that ignored the lives and histories of African Americans in the South. Smith longs for a record of her ancestors' thoughts, wishes and memories. "How I long to kneel alongside the brawl of their voices, the throes of their living. But when I try piecing together the branches of my kin, what I find at so many turns are questions. The absence and silence into which they have been made to disappear arrives to me now as grief. But there was—there surely still somehow is—more."[7]

Smith hopes to carry some of what she learns forward to use it in some way. I also have hope of a use for what I learned from filling the missing narratives with stories and history. And I hope more and more African Americans engage in similar connective work.

While the research and family connections I made helped fill this void with an understanding of my family's journey across generations dating back to the 1840s and 1850s, this history I uncovered is shared by Gullah-Geechee in the region who lived together on cotton plantations in their farming and fishing communities after the Civil War. Nearly half of all the ships carrying enslaved Africans to the United States came in through the port of Charleston, the heart of the Gullah-Geechee region.[8] And while some 260,000 African Americans were believed to be Gullah-Geechee just in the coastal area of George in South Carolina, according to an estimate in 2000, it seems that millions of African Americans are Gullah-Geechee descendants and connected to the culture, given the vast migration of Gullah-Geechee leaving throughout the twentieth century while in search of a better life.[9]

The Gullah-Geechee culture demonstrated that enslaved Africans adapted to America by trying to maintain spiritual concepts, cultural values, the relationships to land and community, food, and language in a nation that devalued it or suppressed it. The very existence of Gullah-Geechee culture is a testament to the resilience of enslaved Africans who shaped it and their descendants who kept it alive. And the fact that three of my ancestors served with the US Colored Troops is part of a collective history as well. Nearly 180,000 Black men served in the army or navy during the Civil War, which means that untold millions of the 40 million African Americans in the United States had ancestors who took the risk of fighting for their liberation.[10] This work grew out of the Black freedom struggle that flourished in the 1960s and '70s as Black people sought to push past the silence and erasure and uncover our past. Understanding the Gullah-Geechee cultural legacy and how they lived and live today can contribute to a larger understanding of what it means to be African American and how we've engaged in cultural preservation not only to survive but to thrive.

Acknowledgments

This book would not have been possible without the support of my good friend and former journalist Michael Duckworth, who told me the information I gathered deserved to be shared in a book.

I am eternally grateful to my Hilton Head relatives Phoebe Driessen, the late Mary Bryant, and Sam Wiley who generously welcomed me, sharing their time and patiently answering my numerous questions about their lives. Without their stories and recounting of family history, this book would be far less thorough and less meaningful.

I thank my parents Shirley and Lawrence Rushing who, transformed by the Black freedom movement of the 1960s, raised me with the belief that our history and our African ancestry mattered deeply.

I thank my grandmother Ruth Pearson, who passed more than a decade before my research began, for sharing stories about Hilton Head and Savannah simply because she knew I cared.

I am grateful to my Cousin Eileen Flowers who accompanied me on trips to Hilton Head and kept in touch with more relatives, North and South, than anyone in the family. I thank her for sharing what she remembered and connecting me to relatives.

I thank Emory Campbell for welcoming me into his home and generously offering his time to talk about life on Hilton Head before the bridge and after, the Gullah-Geechee culture he grew up in, and issues involving land ownership. Emory's openness to talking to me is proof of the connectedness of Gullah-Geechee families in Hilton Head whose ties date back to at least the Civil War era and still hold value today.

Much thanks to Murray Christopher who took me to to the graveyard of Sancho, Adam, and Jacob one day after I arrived in Hilton Head in 2010. Murray shared much of his knowledge and memories of Hilton Head with me.

Thanks to James "Crabman" Green, one of the last of the native islanders who still was cast-net fishing in 2018, for taking me out on his boat.

I am thankful to University of South Carolina Press Acquisitions Editor Ehren Foley who reviewed a portion of this book when it was far less coherent. Fortunately, Ehren saw the possibility of a publishable book in it, which encouraged me to keep working.

I am grateful for the help of Sandra Yin, who edited my manuscript before it was revised. I thank Sandra for the thoroughness of her process and the many helpful suggestions about structure.

I thank my friend and author, Victor Chen, who saw my first attempts to write some of this story and offered honest feedback, which helped me to identify unifying themes to share in this book.

I am thankful to African studies professor Joseph Opala who helped me figure out the likely ethnic origins of my second great-grandfather's name. Joe also spent many hours talking to me about the linguistic and cultural connections between the Gullah-Geechee and the peoples of Sierra Leone.

Much thanks to colleague Chris-Jordan Bloch, who heard about this project and offered his photo editing skills, which definitely enhanced the visual elements of my book.

Much thanks to Dr. Jessica R. Berry for taking time to discuss the Gullah-Geechee Creole with me. And I greatly appreciate B.J. Dennis for sharing so much about the Gullah-Geechee food heritage.

I am grateful to volunteers at the Heritage Library in Hilton Head, especially Rick Bart, who spent years researching the lives of Black Civil War veterans of Hilton Head. Bart and other volunteers pointed to me to records and documents relevant to my ancestors' lives from enslavement to land ownership, farming, and voting in the Reconstruction era.

A huge thanks to my wife, Elena, for all the brainstorming and useful suggestions that I incorporated into this work. I also thank her and my daughters, Maya and Fabiola, for their sacrifices and bearing with me when I was less available than I wanted to be because of the time and energy this book required.

Introduction

In September 2010, Cousin Eileen Flowers and I took a 10-hour drive to Hilton Head, South Carolina. While both of us were New York City transplants who had become Washington, DC, residents, our roots stretched back to this island some 200 years. The trip would change my life.

Eileen was one of a few of my cousins who loved Hilton Head. She usually went back to visit a couple times each year. Back in the 1960s, when she first started to visit the island as an adult, the peacefulness, natural beauty, and simplicity kept calling her back. Hilton Head was so quiet back then that her grandma who lived there knew who was driving when a car passed by on the way to work and when it generally returned. It was far different from Eileen's fast-paced life in Harlem.

On my first visit in 2010, I knew we were getting closer to the island and an area quite different from places where I'd lived as we drove past marshes and creeks, the saw palmetto trees with their distinctive fan-shaped fronds and the trees draped with Spanish moss.

The last time I had been to the island I was a toddler, so I had scant memories of it. This time I'd come with a sense of mission. I wanted to understand my family roots and the journey my ancestors had traveled to emancipation. What were their lives like? And how was their culture more African than most? Were we in fact Gullah-Geechee?

I was hoping to learn about my Great-great-grandfather Sancho Christopher, the ancestor with an African name, who joined the US Colored Troops along with my great-great-grandmother's twin brothers, Adam and Jacob Jenkins. Nobody in my family talked about Sancho, Adam, or Jacob or about the Civil War. And no one talked about enslavement. I would have to search for lost memories, pore over archival and historical records, and push against the silence that had buried our family's past.

On this trip I wanted to meet relatives who stayed in and around Hilton Head and learn about their lives and the Gullah-Geechee culture. I wanted to dredge up memories that relatives had pushed to their mind's corners and bridge whatever gulf the Great Migration had created when just a generation or two ago we were one large family. I wondered what history I would uncover. Would it reveal how African Americans shaped their destiny in the face of oppression?

As we approached Hilton Head, darkness surrounded us. We passed over wetlands and the warm air hung heavy with salt. My connection to this island felt bone deep.

The next morning Eileen asked a distant cousin I'd never met, Murray Christopher, to take us around Hilton Head. She told me he knows a lot about the island and its history and culture.

That day, after a stop at Mitchelville Park, the site of the only self-governing Black town created by the federal government during the Civil War, Murray took us down a gravel-and-dirt road and got out of the car. I wondered what was up. He pointed to a small cluster of tombstones. The steamy South Carolina sun bore down on us like a hot wet blanket, leaving my shirt sticking to my back and huge beads of sweat pouring off my face. I got out and the mosquitoes jumped on my skin as if I were the meal they had been waiting for. As I walked through the tall grass, I saw a small, weathered rose-and-beige head-stone with a shield engraved on it and the following inscription, S. Christopher, Co. E., U.S.C.I., which referred to the United States Colored Infantry, the Black men who enlisted in the Union Army and won their freedom. It seemed Sancho wanted the world to know he had fought for his freedom, and nothing else about his life mattered when he was gone.

I was in shock. Right next to me lay the remains of a man I had wondered about since hearing his African name for the first time as a child. I was confronting history that no one in the family knew anything about. Sancho was not the only relative buried here. Just a few yards away lay the remains of Adam and Jacob Jenkins, his brothers-in-law and my great-great-uncles. Like him, they served in the 21st Regiment of the US Colored Infantry, which in 1865 helped liberate Charleston, after the Confederates set fire to bales of cotton in the city as they fled. In helping to liberate Charleston, the Black troops freed the area around the port where about half of all enslaved Africans entered the United States. Charleston marked the end of a traumatic journey where enslaved Africans would be sold at one of many markets before generations of additional trauma and enslavement began. In this incredible time of celebrations and commemorations, Black Charleston residents removed dead Union soldiers from a mass grave and buried them with honors in a ritual then known as Decoration Day, which would later become Memorial Day. The 21st Regiment would take part in that first Decoration Day.

Adam's and Jacob's headstones were also engraved with shields. Other relatives' headstones stood nearby in this modest Gullah-Geechee graveyard. There was one of my grandmother's older sisters, Julia, the mother of twelve children—some of whom would inform me about the Hilton Head they grew up in before the island was developed. Nearby was Eugene, her son, who had returned to Hilton Head after years up North to open a successful bar and restaurant with his wife.

My second great-grandfather Sancho Christophe's gravesite
in Drayton Cemetery yards from Port Royal Sound.

My daughters (*left to right*) Maya, Fabi and I walking through Drayton cemetery in
2018, visiting the graves of ancestors and relatives.

This graveyard was on land where Sancho, Jacob, and Adam had been enslaved on a 700-acre cotton plantation, known as Fish Haul Creek Plantation or Drayton Plantation. They were buried just yards from the Drayton family mansion that was built at the edge of Port Royal Sound.

The Popes and then the Draytons, families that owned and managed this plantation in the last few years before the Civil War, had built wealth from the toil and confinement of enslaved Africans who grew a type of long-staple cotton known as Sea Island cotton. The Draytons were among the first group of white settlers colonizing South Carolina. The plantation owners' families lived in mansions. They sometimes educated their children in Europe. Their descendants became physicians, politicians, and corporate leaders. They built luxurious lives off the fruits of the labor of my ancestors and other enslaved Africans in Hilton Head and South Carolina's Lowcountry.

I can name six ancestors whose sweat and blood poured into the soil of this former plantation across generations extending back 180 years. As enslaved people, they owned little. As free people with no wealth, they managed to cobble together enough to buy land, create small farms and establish a life in freedom. They had little political power to wield. But they were among a few hundred families that knew how to build homes and boats, grow vegetables, and transport them for sale in Savannah. They could maintain a community, building praise houses, which functioned as Gullah-Geechee centers of religious worship, and schools. They could work hard, hope for a better future, and create greater opportunities for their children. And the bones of many of them still lay on this land, long after the white people who enslaved them left.

Although New York City, my birthplace, was the only city where I could ever feel totally at home, this island felt even more deeply like home. I connected to this physical space, the land, the heat, the pines and palmettos, the tidal creeks and rivers and my ancestors on what feels like a spiritual level in ways I can't fully describe.

Ironically, this feeling existed in a place where the torment of enslavement took place. But generations of ancestors and relatives lived out their lives here. They gave birth here. They raised children here. They played here and prayed here. They fished and farmed here on land they would own after slavery. Although my grandmother and many other relatives had left, the histories of their ancestors would live on and not be erased. The research I was doing would see to it.

The graveyard where Sancho's, Adam's, and Jacob's remains lay is near where freedom began. Just yards away in Port Royal Sound on November 7, 1861, the federal government's naval ships captured a sizable portion of the coast of South Carolina between Charleston and Hilton Head in the Battle of Port Royal. In Hilton Head, Thomas F. Drayton, who was running Fish Haul Plantation and leading rebel forces there, was driven off the island within hours along with other Confederates. The enslaved would live in limbo, considered contraband, until the war's end. But slavery would exist no more.

A few months after President Abraham Lincoln authorized Black troops to fight by signing the Emancipation Proclamation on New Year's Day 1863, Adam, Jacob, and Sancho would enlist, fighting to make sure the Union won, and their freedom would last. Adam would build a house in Mitchelville, the self-governing town created for African Americans by the federal government. All three would get married, own land, run their farms, and also work other jobs to generate income. And they, along with other freedpeople, would help define a lifestyle in autonomous, nearly-all Black Gullah-Geechee communities taking care of themselves, as white people throughout South Carolina began erecting a system of Jim Crow, creating a new form of White supremacy to replace the system of enslavement.

Drayton cemetery is still maintained by my family's church, St. James Baptist, whose origins date back to First African Baptist Church, the first Black church formed on Hilton Head in Mitchelville. The area near the cemetery, now a residential community, bears little resemblance to the plantation where enslaved Africans lived and labored.

The plantation home where the Popes and Draytons lived no longer stands. Island residents are believed to have dismantled it after the Civil War when they needed lumber for construction. But just down the road in an area surrounded by fencing are the remnants of fireplaces that existed on the plantation made with tabby cement. Once common in South Carolina's Lowcountry, the cement was made with lime and oyster shells. The fireplaces were once used to heat cabins on what was called slave row, where more than fifty enslaved people, including my ancestors, lived.

In this area, the present mixes incongruously with the past. While a historical marker notes the significance of the tabby cement ruins, Barker Field, where Little Leaguers play, is just outside the enclosure as if these fireplace remnants have no historical significance. The fact that children are throwing baseballs nearby is at odds with one of the few visible reminders of enslavement on Hilton Head, dishonoring the memories of those whose lives were confined there.

The only structures that remain from Fish Haul Plantation are the tabby cement remnants of fireplaces that the enslaved used to heat their cabins.

The historical marker that mentions the fireplaces highlights the first white settlers in Hilton Head and the white families that owned Fish Haul plantation. It notes that the plantation was part of a 1717 land grant of 500 acres to Colonel John Barnwell who established the first plantation on Hilton Head. Members of the Green, Ellis, and Pope families were later owners. Nearby tabby cement ruins are the remains of slave cabin fireplaces. "Graves of blacks, who made up most of the island's population until after the 1950s, are in nearby Drayton Cemetery," the marker states.

The facts surrounding the lives of the people who lived in those cabins and worked on this plantation, like Sancho, Molly, Adam, and

Historical maker indicating that Fish Haul Plantation was originally part of the first plantation established by colonist Col. John Barnwell through a land grant.

Jacob, remain buried. My family, like so many African American families, did not pass down much of anything about the lives of those ancestors who had been enslaved. Telling some stories about slavery would have been difficult and painful. But along with the pain, there would surely have been stories of heroism, defiance, joy, and laughter to inform descendants of their ancestral past, achievements, and failures, perhaps inspiring those living today. But perhaps the pain was too great to reveal these stories. Yet generations living in recent times who feel this sense of void and emptiness are the ones who need it.

Aunt Aggie, born in 1897, thirty-two years after the Civil War ended, shared a household with her grandparents, Sancho and Molly, while growing up. Although she was about 16 when her grandfather died, she didn't have much to say about him. By the time we talked about the ancestors she could remember in 1977, Aunt Aggie was a gentle and soft-spoken elderly woman. She openly shared the names she knew. I suspect she could have told us more about Sancho and Molly. But for some reason dredging up memories of them must have been difficult.

My grandmother seems to have heard conflicting stories about enslavement in Hilton Head. After "Roots" first aired, she told me that one of our ancestors was like Kunta Kinte, because he repeatedly ran away from the plantation where he was enslaved. And that was the only time anyone in the family ever acknowledged slavery in our past.

Elders taught Grandma when she was growing up that the people of the Sea Islands had not been enslaved but were the descendants of captives on slave ships who jumped from those ships as they approached the shore and swam to the islands where they made a life for themselves as free people. This myth must have been intended to replace difficult memories of slavery with an inspiring origin story.

+ + +

Thanks to Aunt Aggie, I was able to dig deeper into an unknown past than I imagined. By telling me Sancho's name, she gave me an unusual thread to follow. Armed with that name, I could turn to records, documents, and other living relatives to fill the void.

I learned at a workshop on African American genealogy that the National Archives and Records Administration maintained service records of members of the US Colored Troops with information on all who served, including pension files with more about their lives if the veteran applied for a disability pension. The US Pension Bureau was created under the General Act of 1862, passed by Congress, to offer pensions to disabled veterans. But the Dependent and Disability Pension Act of 1890 enabled Civil War veterans who were disabled to receive pensions even if their disability happened after their service. These files provided substantial amounts of information about Black troops as they had to go to great lengths to document their identities, birthplaces, and circumstances relevant to their physical condition with statements from themselves, witnesses, and medical examiners to qualify for benefits.[1]

With time between jobs in 2010 I visited the National Archives and was directed to microfilm that contained the date Sancho enlisted. It was April 4, 1863, just three months after Abraham Lincoln issued his Emancipation Proclamation, freeing the enslaved in the Confederate states that rebelled against the Union. Sancho's military record was a short form that contained a few details: The United States owed Sancho $27.96 in compensation for clothing upon discharge.[2]

Under the remarks section I learned he was detailed as a musician during his three years of service. And Sancho had spent time in the hospital while a soldier, which I later learned was due to contracting smallpox. Next to the word "remarks" on the form was one word: slave. I stared at the word, my eyes widening from the impact. Despite the enormous and incomprehensible weight of slavery, I was glad to find evidence of the truth of his life right before me.

21 | **U.S.C.T.**

Christopher Sancho

Pvt ...., Co. *E*, 21 Reg't U. S. Col'd Infantry.

Appears on **Co. Muster-out Roll,** dated

Charleston, S.C., Apl. 25, 1866 .

Muster-out to date *Apl. 25,* 1866 .

Last paid to *June 30,* 1865 .

Clothing account:

Last settled *Apl. 24,* 186*5* ; drawn since $........ $\overline{100}$

Due soldier $ *27.56/100* ; due U. S. $...........$\overline{100}$

Am't for cloth'g in kind or money adv'd $........$\overline{100}$

Due U. S. for arms, equipments, &c., $ ....$\overline{100}$

Bounty paid $........ $\overline{100}$; due $...........$\overline{100}$

Remarks : *Slave.*

Book mark *1.167. P.97.73. 2200.83-155.{ 125.}*

O. T. Taylor

(861). *Copyist.*

A military record showing that Sancho Christopher had been enslaved and the amount of money he was owed upon discharge.

My family's connection to slavery was obvious. Enslavement of people from West and Central Africa was the means through which the ancestors of almost all African Americans had come to America and become American. But where was the actual evidence of it in my family? I didn't know who had lived through enslavement or where it had happened because no one living knew anything about it. Only by researching Sancho's life would I learn the names of my enslaved ancestors and the first generation to transition from enslavement to liberation.

Days later, in Sancho's disability pension file, I learned more. A member of the Pope family in Hilton Head, South Carolina, was Sancho's enslaver. The woman who would become Sancho's wife, Margaret "Molly" Jenkins, who my grandmother remembered from her early childhood, was also enslaved, like Sancho, along with her siblings and mother at a cotton plantation known by two names, Fish Haul Creek Plantation and Drayton Plantation.

Through these records and a subsequent trip to Hilton Head's Heritage Library History and Ancestry Research Center, I learned the names of nearly one dozen ancestors who lived part of their lives in slavery before the Civil War. The library was engaged in their own research of the lineages of members of the US Colored Troops from Hilton Head. The research didn't lead me to an ancestor who was born in Africa as I originally hoped. Sancho was born in Hilton Head in 1843. But despite the absence of a direct ancestral link to Africa, I found a deeper cultural connection to Africa through our family's Gullah-Geechee heritage than I ever knew existed.

Who Are the Gullah-Geechee?

The Gullah-Geechee are descendants of enslaved Africans from West and Central Africa who were brought to the Atlantic coast and coastal islands in the South. They speak an English-based Creole, derived from contact between West Africans and the British during the eighteenth century. It combines mostly English words with African grammar, structure, and pronunciation.[3]

The relative isolation of the Gullah-Geechee—particularly in the coastal islands of South Carolina, Georgia, and Florida, in spaces only boats could reach from the mainland—enabled them to retain aspects of their African cultures of origin and infuse it with new ways of being that are evident in cuisine; music; spiritual beliefs; folktales; crafts; and concepts of family, kinship, and land ownership.[4]

Like many Gullah-Geechee, my relatives did not use the terms "Gullah" or "Geechee" to describe themselves, probably in part because their unique Creole, food, and beliefs made them vulnerable to ridicule, particularly among other African Americans who found them odd. Geechee, I learned, was widely used to describe Sea Island residents in that region. But it was a loaded term, one to avoid because of the negative stereotypes associated with it.

I interviewed Emory Campbell, the Hilton Head native and well-known Gullah-Geechee expert, to learn more about Gullah-Geechee life before the recent decades when the island underwent tremendous change. We talked about how Gullah-Geechee people saw their own identity and the use of the term "Geechee." To be considered a Geechee, he said, meant being subjected to ridicule because of how much rice you consumed, the "funny way" you spoke, and the assumption that you were backward and closer to being African.[5]

The origins of the term "Gullah" are somewhat uncertain—although many think the term derived from the Gola ethnic group in Sierra Leone, where many enslaved Africans in South Carolina originated. The origin of the term "Geechee," is also uncertain but Lorenzo Dow Turner, a linguist who first traced the origin of the Creole to West African languages, theorized that Geechee might have come from the Kissi ethnic group (pronounced "Geezee") that lives in an area where Sierra Leone, Liberia, and Guinea intersect.[6]

Knowledge of Gullah-Geechee cultural and historical contributions and their relevance to African American culture has grown in recent decades. In 2006, Congress designated the historic region where Gullah-Geechee have lived, the Gullah-Geechee Cultural Heritage Corridor, a national heritage area with certain federal protections, after Gullah-Geechee leaders lobbied for it.

How did the Gullah-Geechee culture develop? Scholars point to a number of factors. The area had a higher density of enslaved Africans living mostly among themselves, with less influence from white culture. A larger percentage of enslaved Africans arrived on plantations in this area even after the importation of slaves was outlawed in 1808, due to illegal smuggling, up to almost the beginning of the Civil War.[7] The relative isolation of people in the Sea Islands and nearby coastal communities allowed the culture to flourish, with less pressure to assimilate to white norms. While Gullah-Geechee left the Sea Islands to travel by boat to the mainland, few outsiders came in.[8]

The Gullah-Geechee in the Sea Islands intentionally sought to acquire small farms on former plantation land and build their own communities after the Civil War ended. In contrast to the battle for integration that is associated with the Black freedom struggle of the 1960s, evidence shows the Gullah-Geechee in Hilton Head and elsewhere in the region had a separatist vision for themselves. Historical accounts from the 1860s show this separatist vision of land ownership informed Union General William T. Sherman's Civil Field Order No. 15, which set aside plots of up to forty acres of plantation land that had been seized for failure to pay taxes, to allow for settlement of the newly freed in the Gullah-Geechee region. Although President Andrew Johnson later repealed that wartime field order and allowed former enslavers to reclaim plantation land, a settlement was arranged that prevented freedpeople from being evicted from land where they had been living.[9]

On Hilton Head, where there was a substantial military presence, the federal government decided to hold on to confiscated former plantations in the aftermath of the Civil War instead of allowing homesteading. And many rented land for farming through the US Direct Tax Commission.[10]

I learned that this separatist vision for reconstruction that emerged during the Civil War in the Gullah-Geechee region was to some extent realized, but it wasn't replicated throughout the South. In many of the more than 100 Sea Islands of South Carolina, Georgia, and Florida, including Hilton Head, Gullah-Geechee people lived in self-contained, self-sustaining communities largely amid the presence of few white people without the daily humiliation of Jim Crow. In Hilton Head, the Gullah-Geechee lived mostly without police or law enforcement, largely policing themselves, according to those I interviewed.

The story of the people of Hilton Head and other islands of St. Helena, Daufuskie, Lady's Island, Port Royal, John's Island, Wadmalaw, and the many inland coastal communities is not a story of passive actors who just happened to live amid deep concentrations of other Black people because of their isolation. These people chose to live among themselves and own their own land. Even when they left for periods to earn additional income, they would return to their farms, wetlands, and creeks where they'd live in kinship-based compounds for generations.[11]

They were able to achieve something rare for African Americans in the United States, creating Black space by choice—free of the "Whites only" signs, the terrorism of the Ku Klux Klan, and lynchings that Black folks throughout the South faced. But the reality of white supremacy and oppression was not distant. It would confront Gullah-Geechee when they left their island communities to take seasonal and temporary jobs, brought their produce to market, and lost their voting rights in the post-Reconstruction era.

The Gullah-Geechee Lowcountry Resources Report, which was developed as part of the process to establish the corridor, notes that it would be exceedingly difficult to estimate the number of Gullah-Geechee in coastal regions of South Carolina and Georgia, given the significant out-migration of Gullah-Geechee that occurred through-out the twentieth century because of the need for economic opportunities. In addition, the South saw an increase of African Americans who aren't Gullah-Geechee moving into the area from northern cities because of decreased job opportunities in the 1970s and a reverse migration. But the report's authors estimated the number of Gullah-Geechee in South Carolina and Georgia to be roughly between 170,000 and 263,000 in 2005.[12]

✦ ✦ ✦

As I learned about my family's past, different aspects of my research filled the void in various ways. The puzzle pieces I put together offered up the past and the present differently and filled parts of the void. Archival records with the statements from my ancestors told me where they were enslaved and what their lives were like after liberation. It's like I could hear their voices through the difficult to read handwritten cursive of the people they spoke to.

My oldest relatives living in Hilton Head told me about the fishing and farming lifestyle, their education, and Gullah-Geechee spirituality as well as what they remember about my grandmother and great-grandmothers and other relatives who went North.

The land, where my ancestors lived and loved, laughed and cried and gave birth to future generations spoke to me too. Not in words but in a way that was soulful and bone deep.

I would learn that I was part of an ancestral village, the only one that I will probably ever have.

When I met strangers and mentioned that my family was from Hilton Head, smiles would spread across their faces, and they'd immediately ask who my relatives were. If they didn't immediately recognize the names, they would ask what church they went to and feel connected. I felt welcomed into an extended family, this kinship among Hilton Head's Gullah-Geechee families with bonds dating back to enslavement: a shared history of families living together for generations, depending on one another and building community together on the same island in similar ways.

The visits helped me understand the Gullah-Geechee culture that developed during slavery that Sancho and Molly were immersed in and continued with the cousins I interviewed. At St. James Baptist, the family church, I was warmly welcomed on Father's Day even though I was a stranger to them; I received a small gift alongside other fathers and was offered a lunch of red rice, jambalaya, and fried chicken. My relationship to cousins Phoebe and Mary made me by extension part of the community.

I would learn the names of people who were well-known in Hilton Head in the early decades of the twentieth century. Nancy Christopher, one of the island's legendary midwives, had ushered many family members into the world. She was born during enslavement and married my great-great-uncle Adam. Many relatives would mention Dr. Willie Aiken, not a physician, but a root doctor who healed the sick when there were no medical doctors on the island. Dr. Aiken was a cousin relatives told me. But I don't know how he was related.

Life in Hilton Head, until about the mid-twentieth century, lacked modern conveniences like electricity, indoor plumbing, paved roads, and phones. There were no doctors or high schools. Life was difficult. But Black people made a living, building their own homes and boats for their fishing and farming lifestyle. Men, I would learn, often worked during the week in Savannah to earn money and then returned on weekends by boat to help their wives and children on the farm.

Upward mobility, skills, and education were difficult for Black people everywhere to access. People would have to leave the island life behind to earn more income, gain access to modern conveniences, and attain a typical middle-class lifestyle. That history of leaving the region for better economic and educational opportunities was reflected in my own family with some relatives staying close while many others went North for good. Others, who were born in Hilton Head, did a reverse migration and returned after decades away. My grandmother and other relatives in New York were among those who left with no plan of ever returning. The socioeconomic benefits are clear, not that all relatives did well financially. But the costs of the ruptures and disconnection with the family were also clear.

While the isolation of the Sea Islands has been credited with helping the culture survive over the decades, that separate life was not to last. Hilton Head began changing at a much faster pace after 1956 when developers inked a deal to build a bridge to the mainland. Most of the island that was not being cultivated by Black people was purchased by white men with access to capital in several transactions. And on that land, they privatized vacation, resort, and retirement communities for mostly white newcomers behind locked gates with their own resources.

The Gullah-Geechee of Hilton Head are now a small minority of the population, and the cultural loss has been substantial, according to those I interviewed. The food and language are still there, and kinship-based family compounds exist to an extent. But the opportunity to understand and learn about the culture as it existed in the first half of the twentieth century before the influx of outsiders is dwindling as more elders, who were closer to the old ways, pass on.

CHAPTER 1

The Rice Connection

Cousin Kitty's red rice at holiday get-togethers. Uncle Green's tata poon (sweet potato pone). The okra gumbo Grandma whipped up after I told her I didn't like okra. These were all distinctive Gullah-Geechee dishes that showed up at holiday gatherings even four or five decades after my grandmother and two of her sisters, Aunt Mabel and Aunt Aggie, left Hilton Head. Gullah-Geechee cuisine includes what we think of as traditional African American soul food. On holidays, when relatives from various households would get together at cousin Kitty's, we might have fried chicken, collard greens and ham hocks, black-eyed peas and rice, corn bread, pig feet or pig ears alongside the red rice and tata poon. In addition to all that, there was typical American holiday food, like roasted turkey, baked ham, and mashed potatoes and gravy.

I was unaware of the origin of Gullah-Geechee dishes in the 1970s and '80s while growing up. But in researching the lives of Sancho and his wife Molly, her twin brothers Adam and Jacob, and the culture they were raised in, I learned of the cuisine's deep West African connections from black-eyed peas and other cowpeas, like red peas, that originated in Africa to the use of peanut and benne or sesame seeds, and okra. Not only did actual foods make the journey from West Africa to America during the transatlantic slave trade, but so did some of the foodways, including cooking styles, recreating the flavors and textures of foods from the homelands of our enslaved ancestors.[1] Through reinvention, Indigenous New World foods, like corn and tomatoes, were incorporated into Gullah-Geechee cuisine. I would learn that rice is thought of as the most significant African contribution to the cuisine. Rice is a primary staple for Gullah-Geechee, reflecting where many of the enslaved in South Carolina originated: West Africa's rice-farming region along the Gambia River, which includes Senegal, Guinea, Guinea-Bissau, and Sierra Leone.[2]

Rice was grown for many centuries in West Africa. In fact, one of only two types of domesticated rice in the world was first domesticated in the wetlands of the middle Niger River in Mali near the Sahara millennia ago. In Timbuktu and Jenne-Jeno, urban centers of Mali, archaeologists have found that rice was being grown as far back as 300 A.D.[3] Chef and culinary historian Michael Twitty dates the cultivation of rice to an even earlier period. "Rice had been a part of West African life in Upper Guinea and the Western Sudan for nearly two thousand years by the time Europeans arrived, spreading out from the heartlands along Senegal, Gambia and Niger Rivers."[4]

Rice was brought with the enslaved who would grow and harvest it for their own sustenance after 1670 when South Carolina was colonized.[5] Between the 1690s and 1720s, rice cultivation took on increasing prominence as an export crop as plantation owners exploited the knowledge and labor of the enslaved for the complex job of growing it. Plantation owners had no experience cultivating it nor the agricultural knowledge to adapt rice grain to South Carolina's climate, according to Judith Carney, who has researched the African food legacy in the Americas. In *Black Rice,* Carney discusses the agricultural contributions of Africans, including various methods of cultivation for different climates from extremely arid to extremely humid: "Through their cultivation of rice, slaves reinforced an African identity by adapting a favored dietary staple of West Africa to tropical and subtropical America."[6] But despite their agricultural knowledge and the brutal labor they were subjected to so as to maximize profits, their enslavers would receive the credit. "The enslavement of Africans dehumanized its victims and disparaged their achievements in agriculture and technology," wrote Carney.[7] In fact, the entire cultivation and adaptation of African plants to the Americas was until very recently overlooked because of race and gender biases.[8]

Only two forms or branches of domesticated rice include Oryza Sativa, cultivated in Asia, and Oryza glaberrima, which was grown in Africa, wrote Kim Severson in a *New York Times* article. The glaberrima rice could be grown in gardens and was, initially, a means for the enslaved to sustain themselves. But Sativa, which became known as Carolina Gold, enabled plantation owners to enrich themselves off the broken bodies of the enslaved.[9]

Carney described the "rain-fed" system of rice cultivation in the early 1700s that rotated land use between rice cultivation and cattle raising, which she attributes to the knowledge enslaved Africans brought to South Carolina. As a consequence, plantation owners sought enslaved Africans from the rice-growing regions of West Africa with skills in tending and herding cattle and horses. Planters learned which African regions and ethnicities specialized in rice cultivation, so they sought slaves from those areas and ethnic groups. But to make rice production very profitable, plantation owners had to increase the yield, and the enslaved began growing rice in wetlands that required clearing swamps of vegetation while contending with snakes and insects. They had to build banks of soil, gates to control the flow of water during the cultivation cycle: containing rainwater and releasing it, flooding fields when necessary.[10]

Demand for enslaved labor and knowledge surged. The share of enslaved Africans brought by the British into South Carolina from Senegal, the Gambia, and Sierra Leone, the rice-growing regions more than quadrupled: from 12 percent to 64 percent between the 1730s and 1774. Some 58,000 enslaved Africans were brought into South Carolina during the 25-year period from 1750 to 1775.[11]

Rice was central to the South Carolina economy, according to Twitty, author of *The Cooking Gene.* In 1850, South Carolina produced more than 100 million pounds of rice, some three-quarters of the nation's output. The Charleston area alone grew nearly half the country's rice.[12]

Africans not only knew how to grow the rice in the wetlands of South Carolina's coastal regions but knew how to process it, including milling it to remove the outer husk and bran from the edible kernel. The work of rice processing was grueling. The enslaved had to mill rice in two periods, one before sunrise and one after sunset, lifting a pestle that weighed as much as ten pounds and smashing it on top of rice husks repeatedly for hours at a time to separate the husk from the grain. High rates of death were attributed to this labor.[13]

Rice is a key part of cultural identity throughout much of West Africa. And for groups who eat rice as a regular part of their diet, a meal without rice is akin to not eating at all, according to Twitty. Rice is the staff of life for them. It is the first solid food eaten as an infant in rice-growing regions of West Africa and the last food before death. Rice grains are offered to the ancestors.[14]

Even how the rice is cooked in the Gullah-Geechee culture reflects roots in West Africa where rice farming was common, according to Wilbur Cross and Eric Crawford. In *Gullah Culture in America,* they describe rice-pot cooking. "The first ingredient, of course, is always rice—whether white, brown, or otherwise—hence the tradition known as the "rice pot" for that treasured (and often antique) vessel in which just about everything is cooked. Following that, almost anything in the larder, fresh or otherwise, can follow, such as vegetables, seafood, chicken, ham, bacon, nuts, and of course a variety of spices."[15]

For the Gullah-Geechee, common rice dishes include red rice, shrimp and rice, crab rice, collard greens and rice, jambalaya, and perlau. Red rice, for instance, is cooked with sausage, bacon, and sometimes shrimp, onions, green bell pepper, or celery and tomato paste. Shrimp rice includes rice, shrimp, and pork neck bones. Some dishes are variations on African recipes. Hoppin' John is black-eyed peas and rice cooked together along with pork. It is a variation of black-eyed peas of Senegal, and waakye eaten in Ghana. When I went to Ghana in 2017 and ordered Waakye, it reminded me of day-old black-eyed peas that had begun to dry out.

Other African dishes seem nearly the same as Gullah-Geechee recipes. Jollof rice, a Senegalese rice dish made with tomatoes and onions, is eaten widely throughout West Africa and is very similar to red rice, which some have referred to as its culinary cousin. The ingredients are similar, and both dishes use less water than standard American cooking, giving the rice a drier texture. Jollof rice, whose name originated with Senegal's Wolof Empire, binds West Africans from different countries together across national boundaries, according to Twitty, and sparks arguments over which version—Senegalese, Sierra Leonean, Ghanaian, or Nigerian—is best. A transnational dish, jollof rice, has spread as West African migrants moved around the world, taking their heritage food with them.[16]

Senegalese cuisine provides a clear example of the centrality of rice within the cultures there. Twitty ticked off Senegalese dishes— rice and chicken, rice and lamb or beef, rice and fish and vegetables, rice with peanut stew, rice with okra or leafy greens. Just like many Gullah-Geechee dishes, rice envelops the meat, seafood, and vegetables in a plate or bowl for a complete meal.

Although Carolina Gold—the rice that plantation owners grew wealthy on—originated in Asia, a red-hulled rice called *hill rice*, possibly West African in origin, was a staple in Southern cooking. It could be grown in a field or garden and did not need the wetter, marshy areas that the more profitable Carolina Gold required.

In Hilton Head, long staple or Sea Island Cotton is what enslavers wrung profits from throughout the 1800s. But rice was grown there. According to the agricultural census of 1868, just three years after the Civil War ended, my great-great uncles grew rice on their small farms, and I suspect they grew hill rice. Jacob Jenkins used one-quarter acre on his 7¼-acre farm that year to produce two bushels of rice. Adam Jenkins used half an acre on his 8½-acre farm to produce five bushels of rice. Unlike the cotton they most likely grew to sell at market, I suspect the relatively small amount of rice they grew was for their families' consumption.

I never thought of the amount of rice in my diet in connection to my ancestry until I learned about the African origin and prominence of rice in the Gullah-Geechee diet.

Rice was a staple in my house, eaten most days. Potatoes or noodles would sometimes accompany a meat dish. But rice was the most common. For years, when my paternal grandmother, from Jamaica, shared a home with my parents, rice-and-peas (either kidney beans or Congo peas) accompanied meat dishes and sides of vegetables all the time. She might cook a big pot of rice and peas on the weekend that we'd eat from for days. For my parents who were busy working, white rice was the norm. But on holidays, Hoppin' John or stewed black-eyed peas and rice was expected. Rice was a central part of my Caribbean and Gullah-Geechee heritage for the same reason: it is what our enslaved West African ancestors grew, ate, and passed down.

The rice-farming region of Africa shows up not only in the prominence of rice in my diet because of my cultural heritage, but also in my DNA, which shows clear connections to rice-growing regions of Africa. According to African ancestry, my maternal lineage links me to the Guinea-Bissau's Brame or Balanta people, rice farmers, who suffered through hundreds of years of the transatlantic slave trade. DNA analysis from Ancestry.com and 23andme shows a genetic connection to Senegambia. I would even learn that Sancho's name is Susu, an ethnic group which grew rice and lives in Sierra Leone and Guinea.

I interviewed retired African Studies professor Joseph Opala,

who spent decades in Sierra Leone and studied the linkages between the Creoles spoken by Gullah-Geechee and the people of
Sierra Leone to deepen my understanding of linguistic and cultural
connections. The essential role rice plays in the diet of both groups
came up in our conversations. Opala recounted how on his first visit
to Campbell's family compound, Campbell nearly apologized about
the amount of rice that might be served. He said Campbell pointed
out the house where his mother was born as they were driving up
and said: "Now I've got to tell you something about being Gullah-
Geechee: We eat rice for breakfast, we eat rice for lunch, and we eat
rice for dinner."

Opala erupted in laughter, he said, telling Campbell he knew
exactly where that statement was going before he finished because
he had heard it many times said the exact same way in Sierra Leone,
where people often feel they must apologize to prepare outsiders for
the frequency of rice in their dishes.

The amount of rice the Gullah-Geechee eat provoked ridicule
among African Americans outside the culture—hence the disparaging expression, "rice-eating Geechee." The love of rice is part of
the stigma they live with. While I didn't hear much ridicule of rice
in connection with the Gullah-Geechee growing up in Queens, New
York, I do remember an elderly neighbor from South Carolina who
would tease his grandson, Keith, about loving rice. The man would
laugh repeatedly and say: "Keith loves rice. Keith eats rice like a
Geechee." Clearly, the teasing was funny to my neighbor but got no
response from Keith who grew up in Maryland, where such ridicule
was meaningless.

Although the centrality of rice is unmistakable, there's a lot
more to Gullah-Geechee cuisine than rice. I talked with Charleston chef B. J. Dennis, an expert on Gullah-Geechee cuisine, and he
emphasized other aspects of the cuisine that are overlooked and
less widely known.[17] "Being by the water meant there was lots of
seafood, fish, lots of fresh oysters, okra, lots of chili peppers, lots of

greens. Greens all year round. Turnip greens, mustard, and collard greens," he told me.

Dennis researches heritage foods that are less common nowadays among the Gullah-Geechee. Some traditional dishes and foodways have gotten lost, he explained, given the dependence on processed foods, including fast food. There are fewer vegetables in the Gullah-Geechee diet than there were for older generations, Dennis said. And, he believes, consumption of meat and bleached white rice is excessive. "The same lima beans and black-eyed peas are still being grown, but everyone wants macaroni and cheese and fried chicken." From farmers in rural areas and people who are in their 90s, Dennis has learned how diverse the Gullah-Geechee diet really was. Wild game was a large part of the cuisine. People ate deer, marsh hens, quail and duck, duck eggs, and guinea hens, he said. While many associate black-eyed peas with southern food, he said, people in the Gullah-Geechee community ate some thirty different kinds of peas, including dixie peas, butter peas, Sea Island red peas, crowder peas, and purple peas. Dennis has described how his grandfather, who was also Gullah-Geechee, grew sugarcane and how they would dry shrimp and fish. They'd pick a fruit that grew on palm trees, making preserves and wine with it. People also had banana and coconut trees that aren't seen much anymore. Aspects of Gullah-Geechee cuisine during the period of enslavement, wrote Twitty, were different from what is now described as Gullah-Geechee cuisine: "Gullah-Geechee folks loved sun-dried seafood, shark, and food drenched in hot pepper and partook of wild fruits and gator tails with relish and, in the earliest days of slavery, also millet and sorghum brought from Africa and Barbados."[18]

Dennis is an ambassador of Gullah-Geechee cooking and foodways and lifts up the cuisine, not only for its taste and African connection, but also for its nutritional value. Our Gullah-Geechee ancestors understood the nutritional properties of the food they ate, said Dennis, and didn't need to learn about veganism to eat in a healthy way. "Our elders knew you couldn't eat certain greens raw," he said. "You have to cook it to get nourishment from it." Dennis hopes to develop a demonstration kitchen to teach single moms and others in South Carolina about this heritage. He wants to see more Gullah-Geechee people returning to the land and farming again, incorporating agriculture in school curriculums to impart their knowledge to new generations of young children.

Cousin Phoebe's Recipe for Red Rice

The Gullah-Geechee cook two kinds of red rice: oven-baked red rice and the stove-top version. Cousin Phoebe cooks hers in a pot on the stove. She learned the stove-top approach watching her mother, Aunt Julia (my grandmother's sister), cook it. Phoebe uses no measuring cup when cooking it and gauges the amount of ingredients to add by looking at what she's adding and relying on memory. She samples the dish as it nears completion to make sure it's ready. My wife and I came up with the measurements while cooking together with her in 2018.

Cousin Phoebe's rice was amazingly good. I must admit that I've struggled to get the same result as we did then while using such a low water-to-rice ratio.

Ingredients

3 slices of thick sliced bacon

2 smoked sausage links or 1 link of kielbasa

2 stalks of celery

1 small yellow onion

4 cups of rice

Roughly 4 cups water (enough to make 5 cups of sauce
    when combined with tomato paste)

1 can of tomato paste (6 ounce can)

2 teaspoons of sugar

Salt and pepper to taste

(Optional) 1 bell pepper and/or shrimp

Directions

Dice the onions, celery, bacon, sausage, and (optional) bell pepper.

Brown the diced bacon and sausage in a large pot.

Add in the onions, celery, bell pepper, and (optional) shrimp.

Add tomato paste and stir.

Add water and rice and continue stirring the mixture until blended.

Reduce heat to lowest flame possible and cover pot.

Stir pot every 10 to 15 minutes to make sure water is absorbed evenly.

Approximate cooking time: 55 minutes.

Note. Unlike traditional boiled rice, this rice steams slowly.

Author with Cousin Phoebe cooking red rice together in the summer of 2018.

CHAPTER 2

A State Rooted in Slavery

❈

To understand the formation of the Gullah-Geechee community in Hilton Head, I sought to understand how social and historical forces and the physical environment influenced life there, shaping it in unique ways.

Part of the context I learned when examining the history of South Carolina is that the colonization of South Carolina is inseparable from enslavement. Unlike other states in the South, like Georgia, in South Carolina the system of slavery was fully embraced from the very beginning. Charleston was established in 1670 and by the middle of the decade, one quarter of the newcomers were enslaved.[1]

Both Indigenous groups and enslaved Africans were victims of forced displacement, the Africans from another continent and the Indigenous from their own land. Indigenous people were burdened with the additional trauma of battling for their lives and the land they had lived on while trying to save their communities from destruction. Indigenous ethnic groups in the region had been contending with colonization efforts from the Spanish and French for decades before the English colonized South Carolina and their population had dwindled through violence and vulnerability to disease.[2]

Carolina, which would later be split into two states, was colonized by the English in 1663 when King Charles gave land to eight members of the nobility, known as Lords Proprietors, in exchange for their loyalty to the British Crown during the English Civil War. The proprietors established the colony as a profit-seeking settlement and studied Barbados's sugar plantation economy, with the aim of replicating that wealth in the Carolinas. At the time, Barbados had the wealthiest sugar plantation economy in the world. Thus, the Lords Proprietors recruited Barbadian plantation owners to help colonize the land, many of whom brought enslaved Africans with them. Initially, the settlers tried to make profits from olives, grapes, and other crops without success. But by 1690, they found that rice agriculture, which, as mentioned earlier, depended on the labor and skills of enslaved Africans, would generate the wealth they sought.[3]

Enslavement was incentivized by the Lords Proprietors as they colonized Carolina. They created a governing document, the Fundamental Constitution of Carolina that offered a vision for the colony, which included offering every landowner twenty acres of land for every enslaved male they imported to the Carolinas and ten acres for every enslaved female. The colonizers sought to enshrine white supremacy in law, stating that every freeman had "absolute power and authority over his negro slaves."[4]

Meanwhile, Indigenous groups—including the Yamasees, Kiawah, Stono, Edisto, Tuscarora, and Wando—had been surviving through trade with English colonizers and military alliances. The English began enslaving Indigenous North Americans, selling them to enslavers in the Caribbean and white landowners in Carolina. The Yamasee began living in Hilton Head and other islands of Port Royal Sound, including St. Helena, and Parris Islands in 1683 after fleeing the Spanish colonization of Georgia. The Spanish destroyed Yamasee communities on those islands in 1686, and the Yamasee moved closer to Charles Town (Charleston). The Yamasee began living in the Hilton Head area again in the 1690s.[5]

The Yamasee were trying to fend off several attacks on their existence simultaneously: the physical colonization of their land, violent attacks, and enslavement while trying to figure out a way to sustain themselves. By 1715, when the Yamasee War broke out, roughly 25 percent of the enslaved in South Carolina were Indigenous. Among the Yamasee, as many as 51,000 were enslaved between 1670 and 1715. The English used Yamasee to embark on slave raids, attacking other Indigenous groups. When the Yamasee War erupted, hundreds of Yamasee fought with hundreds of members of the Carolina militia—half of whom were enslaved Africans.[6]

Some thought the colony might not survive. However, by 1717, the war was considered over, and Yamasee would begin moving back to Florida. To reduce tension and the possibility of violent conflict, colonizers began reducing reliance on enslaving Indigenous people while focusing increasingly on bringing in enslaved people from the Caribbean and later Africans directly from the continent. Some of the enslavers who would grow enormous wealth from rice plantations, including the Middletons and Draytons, emigrated from Barbados during the founding of Charleston.[7] (Thomas Fenwick Drayton, a descendant of the first Draytons to emigrate to Charleston, and his children were the last owners of Fish Haul Plantation where my enslaved ancestors lived before the Civil War.)

The history surrounding the creation of a state fueled by enslaving people, both Indigenous and Black, is the truth that contrasts with the narrative we all learn of Europeans coming to America seeking religious and political freedom and better economic opportunities. While seeking religious and political freedom and economic opportunities were drivers of English settlement, the Carolinas were born through settler colonialism, the conquest of Indigenous people and seizure of their land, and the enslavement of Africans to build power and wealth among English elites. Their vision of freedom was dependent on my ancestors' confinement. As I began to understand how the Gullah-Geechee culture emerged, its formation seemed inseparable from enslavement. In fact, the merging of cultures from West Africa, the Creole language, spirituality, and sense of justice that defined the culture were responses to slavery's oppressiveness and dehumanization. Our ancestors resisted the harms of enslavement through the culture they created affirming the value of their own lives.[8]

One distinctive aspect of South Carolina's Lowcountry up through the Civil War was the much higher concentration of enslaved Africans and their descendants and the small percentage of white people, enabling the enslaved to form and pass down a more African culture than was possible in other parts of the South. Furthermore, the illegal slave trade continued to bring enslaved Africans and their cultural influences directly from Africa up until 1858, right before the Civil War.[9]

Unlike most of the nation, South Carolina had a Black majority by 1708, early in the colony's history. By 1740, there were twice as many Blacks in South Carolina as white people. In 1860, a few years before the start of the Civil War, 81 percent of the population was enslaved.[10] The ratio of slaves to white people on plantations in South Carolina was typically about 50:1.[11] The Black-to-white ratio in the Sea Islands was even higher. Few white people stayed on Sea Island plantations during the warm weather months, from March to November, given the heat, humidity, and mosquitoes carrying malaria. Overseeing the plantations was left to a "driver" who was usually Black. In the Beaufort District, 25 percent of plantations would operate without any white presence, according to a review of census records from 1790 to 1820.[12]

According to Kytle and Roberts: "Planter absenteeism, geographic isolation, and the regular infusion of new slaves contributed to a greater degree of African cultural retention in the Lowcountry than in other North American slave societies." The lack of whites and greater autonomy impacted the development of the culture of the enslaved in the Lowcountry. "The most obvious example of this phenomenon," they wrote, "was the emergence of Gullah—the syncretic language and culture of the coastal South Carolina slaves crafted from African and New World elements."[13]

The Gullah-Geechee also developed a heritage of cultivating land for their own benefit during enslavement. They labored under a "task system"—utilized in the Caribbean—that allowed them some ability to use their time as they chose after they completed their task, the daily work duties required of them. Sometimes they grew vegetables for their own consumption on small quarter-acre plots and tended to the crops after their task was completed. To a small extent they could farm for themselves, which enabled them to maintain a positive connection to the land.[14]

The period of enslavement would begin in Hilton Head when Colonel John Barnwell was given a 1,500-acre land grant in 1717 and Myrtle Bank plantation was established. Fish Haul Plantation was partitioned from Myrtle Bank. Sixteen families would dominate Hilton Head's 30,000 acres until the Civil War. And while the enslaved grew other crops, long-staple cotton also known as Sea Island cotton would help plantation owners build greater wealth.

Long-staple cotton, grown from seeds that originated in the Caribbean, were more highly valued and more profitable than the typical short-staple cotton grown throughout the South because of its much longer, silkier fibers. Beaufort District, where Hilton Head is located, was generating great wealth from long-staple cotton production. Per capita income there was more than three times the national average in 1861. Cotton was essential to the US economy. Sixty percent of the nation's exports at the start of the Civil War consisted of cotton sales, and cotton contributed $200 million to the economy each year. Fish Haul Plantation, where my ancestors labored, exemplified the conditions needed for profitably growing long-staple cotton in Hilton Head.[15] Visitors to Fish Haul would see acres of cotton plants growing three to four feet, the plantation's oak trees and the dozen cabins referred to as slave row.

But with the start of the Civil War, the Sea Island cotton plantation economy that helped build owners' riches would crumble. Black people, including Sancho, Adam, and Jacob, would turn the war from a conflict to preserve the union to a war of liberation. They would be the first generation of enslaved Gullah-Geechee that got to live most of their lives in liberation, no longer bound to the land as property. In the 1840s when Sancho was born, the idea of the enslaved owning land must have been inconceivable to their enslavers who would fight to keep them in bondage as human tools, the engines of their plantation-based wealth. The Gullah-Geechee were legally bought and sold as chattel, like cows and goats, farm tools, or produce. I do not know what Sancho or Molly's daily life was like during slavery or what horrors they may have witnessed. But I learned something about the conditions.

Slave cabins in the Sea Islands were generally 14 × 20 feet, and housed at least two families, which would mean they would lack any privacy, forced to lie shoulder to shoulder with virtually no space between sleeping bodies at night. The cabins were built in such a way that Fish Haul's owners could always keep watch over the enslaved.[16]

The brutality of slavery in Hilton Head seems invisible now. But some oral accounts reveal horrific trauma the enslaved experienced there. One account passed down through oral history revealed the presence of a tabby cement table, called a Banju, where the enslaved were sometimes sold away from their families. Public beatings happened as well.[17] In my own research, I found that my great-grandmother's husband, Moses Polite, who had lived on a plantation in nearby Bluffton, had been separated from his father when an estate was settled and property was divided. And my third Grandmother Benis (Venus) seems to have been the victim of sexual exploitation, most likely by an owner or his family member. Day-to-day, the Gullah-Geechee of the Sea Islands were forced to toil in the intense heat and humidity of South Carolina summers amid yellow fever and malaria, while white plantation owners who lived lives of luxury generated through enslavement would flee for the greater comfort of their spacious mansions from March to November.[18]

Despite the exploitation and dispossession from their cultures of origin, enslaved Africans made sense of the world they were thrust into. The memories they brought would be maintained in some ways and also developed and reshaped into a new unique Gullah-Geechee culture that would show up in the language they spoke; the foods they ate; the way they worshiped and connected to spirit; and their communal culture, system of justice, and concepts of land owner-ship. Perhaps the community and culture they developed provided some consolation for their anguish, a sense of shared struggle for their alienation and some joy when they could find it.

CHAPTER 3

What's in a Name?

In 1990, a research team discovered an elderly Gullah-Geechee woman, Mary Moran, in coastal Georgia who could sing an ancient funeral hymn in the Mende language of Sierra Leone. Her family had passed the song down through generations for 200 years.

It was a significant discovery, considering how most African Americans cannot claim any cultural artifacts passed down directly from their African ancestors. To be able to claim a connection to the language and words of one's African ancestors is a privilege. As I researched my family's roots, I discovered more details about my ancestry than I could ever have expected.

To get a better sense of the world my ancestors inhabited and who they were, I tried to understand the origin of the African names in my family dating back some 200 years. I wondered what the names meant to my Gullah-Geechee ancestors and why it was important to pass them down in a nation that did not seem to value anything African aside from the labor of their bodies and their agricultural expertise.

However, I would learn that the Gullah-Geechee held native-born Africans in high esteem during enslavement because of the spiritual knowledge they carried from Africa. For the Gullah-Geechee, being African did not carry the stigma and negative associations that it did for many African Americans who had less power to control their images and had a greater propensity to internalize the racist ideas of white society.

I would never learn whether Sancho knew something about the ethnic origins of his ancestors and whether his name was a reflection of his identity. But I could consult experts who have studied the Gullah-Geechee culture, language, and naming traditions. One key resource was the work of Lorenzo Dow Turner, a professor of English and linguistics who conducted research in the 1940s identifying African names from thirty-two languages and ethnic groups used by the Gullah-Geechee. He traced the names to the regions of West and Central Africa where the words existed in languages of specific groups. Often, he found that Gullah-Geechee names were used as personal names in Africa, but he also found Gullah-Geechee names that might have been the words used for specific objects, or adjectives or attributes in the languages of African ethnic groups. Turner identified Sancho's name as possibly Temne or Mende, which are two of the largest ethnic groups in Sierra Leone. He also found Sancho's name in the Hausa language of Nigeria.[1]

After I began the research in 2010, it was deeply moving to find Sancho's name among the 4,000 names and words Turner identified. To learn more about the possible origin of Sancho's name I reached out to Joseph Opala, an African studies professor who lived for decades in Sierra Leone and researched the historical, cultural, and linguistic connections between the people there and the Gullah-Geechee. Opala pioneered research that found some 30,000 enslaved Africans departed from Sierra Leone after being held in a slave fort called Bunce Island. Those enslaved Africans were sold between 1670 when Charleston was established and 1807 when the legal slave trade ended.

The peoples of Sierra Leone seem to have had a more pronounced influence on the Gullah-Geechee than other cultures in West Africa, according to Opala, which is likely because most of the enslaved brought to South Carolin and Georgia were coming from what was known as the Rice Coast, which stretched south from Senegal to Sierra Leone and Liberia. Among the thousands of words and personal names used by the Gullah-Geechee, about 25 percent derive from languages spoken in Sierra Leone. All the African songs and prayers in African languages passed down among the Gullah-Geechee were in languages spoken in Sierra Leone, Opala explained, which underscores the influence of Sierra Leone on the Gullah-Geechee Creole.

Over the course of several conversations in 2018, Opala helped me determine that the likely ethnic origin of Sancho's name, spelled Sankoh in Sierra Leone, was Susu or (SouSou), an ethnic group that has a small population in Sierra Leone and a larger population in Guinea. Opala was familiar with the major ethnic groups and their names in Sierra Leone and suspected Susu was the origin. Turner, he explained would have linked the name Sankoh to the Mende and Temne, said Opala, because many Mende and Temne have that name, acquired through intermarriage over hundreds of years. To confirm his hunch about the Susu origins of Sancho, Opala reached out to Dr. Phil Misevich, an historian at St John's University in New York, who specializes in the slave trade and teaches African, Caribbean, and Atlantic History.

Misevich agreed that Sankoh was originally a Susu name and pointed to research from David Skinner, who wrote that a Sankoh family was among six prominent Mande families of the Susu ethnic group that migrated to Sierra Leone in the eighteenth and nineteenth centuries from the area of the Niger River Valley.[2] This migration of families to Sierra Leone was happening as the transatlantic slave trade was bringing millions to the Caribbean and Americas. One Susu family with the last name Sankoh established the Sankoh section in Melikuri town in Sierra Leone and controlled the Melikuri-Kolente area of Sierra Leone. A Mandinka chief with the name Sankoh is said to have seized authority of Port Loko, a trading center between 1750 and 1760. The family dominated Port Loko until 1815.[3]

Judith Carney's research showed that this control of parts of Sierra Leone involving commerce and trade was happening during an intense period of the transatlantic slave trade in the 1700s and 1800s when enslaved Africans were being sought from rice-growing regions to work on plantations in South Carolina.

I asked Opala about the people who used the name Sankoh to learn more about their culture and history. He explained that the Susu had a privileged position in Sierra Leone having been traders and tributaries of the empires of Gala and Mali. The Susu are recognized in the history of African Empires. In 1240, when Ghana was in decline and splintering into separate states, the Susu vied with the Mankdinka, the rulers of the empire of Mali, to dominate trade, which led to a battle between Sumanguru Konte, the Susu King, and Sundiata Keita, the ruler of Mali. The Susu lost.[4]

Ancient Ghana had drawn its wealth in Western Sudan, trading gold and ivory from further south, connecting through trade routes in Mauritania and Morocco to North Africa. As the empire grew, it profited through trade in salt, copper, cotton, kola nuts, and swords and tools from craftsmen in Arabia, Italy, and Germany. It also traded in the bodies of those who had been enslaved.[5]

The emperors of Mali dominated the trade that ancient Ghana controlled, deriving great wealth from import and export duties into Sub-Saharan Africa. And the Susu, who were traders under their dominion, carried the imprint of the Mandinka rulers in their culture and way of life. People who were not Mandinka but lived near them would emulate the Malian style of dress, adopt their military prowess, use the Arabic alphabet to write in their language, and use the Arabic system of accounting for trade, Opala explained.

The Susu were able to colonize part of Sierra Leone because of their military prowess and prominent position as traders and tributaries of the empires of Mali, Opala explained The Susu, who were

Muslim, colonized land as they moved into Sierra Leone and built mosques and schools. The Susu, together with other ethnic groups with traders connected to the Mali Empire, fanned out from the empire's lands over hundreds of years even as the empire declined. The Susu were one of several Mande groups, like the Mandinka, who spoke a Mande language and had linguistic and cultural ties to other Mande groups, which added to their power. Skinner wrote that "The migrants were traders, Muslim missionaries, warriors, adventurers or refugees from war. Often the migrants came in small groups whose members were related through marriage or parentage, and they carried with them common cultural and political ties."[6]

The Susu's history as traders within the Mali Empire gave them a strong position with respect to external trade. They profited off the slave trade in the late eighteenth century as plantation owners in the United States increasingly sought enslaved Africans from Senegambia. "The Susu, Fula, and the Mandinka were dominant groups in the trans-Saharan trade, and those skills were transferable to the slave trade," Opala explained. "They could read and write and knew Islamic law, which was important for trade. And they had all been involved in long-distance trade."[7]

Walter Rodeny noted that the Susu, Fula, and Mandinka were the most active agents of the slave trade in that region of West Africa.[8] Despite the prominent role of the Susu in the slave trade, those groups who raided other ethnic groups and territories to enslave others also experienced retaliatory counterattacks. It is only logical that some Susus would have also fallen victim to slave raids, been sold, and ended up in the Deep South on a rice or cotton plantation, Opala said.

I soon learned that the Susu engaged in so many slave raids that they maintained a sizable portion of enslaved people who became a subset of the Susu with far less privilege. I spoke at length with James Steel Thayer, a former professor of history at Oklahoma State University, who lived among the Susu to study their religious practices.

He described them as "enthusiastic enslavers."[9] The profitability of the transatlantic slave trade drove them to settle in coastal areas of Sierra Leone, he told me. The Susu had a sizable population of enslaved people to do their labor, such as farming, up until 1926 when the League of Nations banned domestic slavery, he said. While domestic slavery no longer exists in Sierra Leone, the Susu are still split between those who are considered "freeborn" and other Susu who are the descendants of the enslaved. And although both groups are phenotypically the same, speak the same language, and have the same surnames, Thayer explained, the descendants of the enslaved are considered an inferior caste. So-called "freeborn" Susu frown on intermarriage with those who are the descendants of the enslaved. Members of the freeborn Susu may refuse to sell any of their land to the descendants of enslaved people because they'd prefer not to have them living among them. The lineages of each group are well-known and the lines to demarcate the privileged from the subjugated are still enforced, Thayer told me.

When I reflect on the origin of the significance of the name Sankoh, the Susu's active involvement in enslavement is deeply troubling. They profited from ripping people away from their mothers, fathers, sisters, and brothers to be chained aboard slave ships where they would lie in their own feces, perhaps dying of disease during the brutal voyage, or jumping overboard to their death in shark-infested waters. The Susu, like the Mandinka and Fulani, like the Yoruba and Igbo of Nigeria, and Fon of Benin, were among many ethnic groups whose history includes participating and seeking profit from the sale of bodies in exchange for goods from Europe, including firearms that were used in wars and slave raids.

There are many truths to hold at the same time when reflecting on the name. Whoever first came to North America bearing the name Sankoh would have been an unfortunate victim of the slave trade, forced to labor in a rice field or cotton plantation. They might not have been personally involved in the trade in captives and even opposed the practice. Or they may have been willing participants in battling other ethnic groups for profit, enslaving those who lost the battle. Perhaps they felt forced to take up arms and participate—and saw no way to avoid it. On the one hand, the name offered a narrative around the history of the Susu: sophisticated Muslim men, building mosques and schools, trading goods from the Arab world, Europe, and Africa, fighting for dominance against the Mandinka over the Mali Empire. And some of the enslaved, perhaps an ancestor of mine, sought to maintain this memory of home and the past.

But on the other hand, there's the Susu's history of profit from the trade in human beings, which created centuries of trauma and dehumanization that African Americans and other members of the African diaspora faced.

The descendants of enslaved Africans in the United States, the Caribbean, and Latin America live daily with a legacy of racism and white supremacy expressed through laws, policies, and social practices and racist beliefs that were established, institutionalized, and interwoven into daily life during the slave trade. And that white supremacy and many forms of racism live with us today. To me, African Americans must grapple with the fact that the Susu and other ethnic groups who sought to benefit from enslavement, have a shared responsibility with Europeans who led the transatlantic slave trade for, the harm it caused.

Nevertheless, by giving Sancho his name, his parents pointed to a heritage, culture, and region that was a source of origin for the Gullah-Geechee and perhaps their own lineage. The name Sancho and the Susu gave me a specific history to understand, beyond the very general narrative that we're descended from Africans from a huge region of West and Central Africa who ended up captured and sold into enslavement. Learning about the name Sankoh and the Susu helped fill the void and blank space I grew up with. But answers often lead to more questions. Did my great-great grandfather Sancho know why his mother Heena and father Prince gave him that name? What did it mean to him? Did he know about the Susu history in Senegambia and the Mali Empire? Did he know about the role the Susu played in enslaving other groups? It seems impossible that I will ever find answers to those questions. Yet the name remains a gift my ancestors left me. If Sancho had had a more typical Anglo name, it would not have nagged at me, stirred my curiosity and called to me to search for answers. I think the name Sancho likely did what my ancestors intended, which was to maintain connections to their ancestral origins, planting a seed for others to learn from. And in so doing it left a path for descendants like me to follow, to learn more about their lives and cultural origins.

Phillip D. Morgan found that enslaved Africans in South Carolina's Lowcountry were more successful in passing on African names than holding on to their own African names when owners' inventories of the enslaved are compared to inventories in Virginia, which had a smaller percentage of native-born Africans than the Lowcountry dating back to the early 1700s. For enslaved Africans, Morgan attributed the passing down of African names to a desire to retain connections to their land and cultures of origin. "This pattern seems clear: although some African immigrants were able to retain their names, more often they bequeathed homeland names to their children in an effort to honor tradition and family ties," he wrote.[10]

The African naming tradition in my family seems to have gone on for at least two generations. Sancho listed his mother's name as Heena on documents for his Freedmen's bank account. Heena is spelled "Hina" in Turner's *Africanisms in the Gullah Dialect.* To spell names, Lorenzo Dow Turner used the international phonetic alphabet that linguists use. Heena was a feminine name that means to be obstinate or press in the Umbundu language of Angola. But he also found the word "Heena" in the Mende language of Sierra Leone; there it wasn't a name but a word for male.[11] If my third great-grandmother, Heena, was of Angolan descent that would also make a lot of sense, since nearly 40 percent of Africans brought to South

Carolina originated in Angola and the Congo.[12] As with Sancho's name, his mother's name leaves me with similar questions about what she may have known about her name and why her parents gave her that name.

Other names in my lineage that are part of the Gullah-Geechee naming tradition may well be African in origin. But it is difficult to be certain because the names have English equivalents. My great-great-grandmother's nickname was Molly, a diminutive of the Hebrew name, Mary, and of Margaret. However, Molly's name might also have been Male (pronounced "Ma-lay") in the universal alphabet linguists use. Turner found Male to be a Fon name that the Gullah-Geechee gave to both girls and boys. The Fon are the largest ethnic group in Benin. Turner also identified Mali (Ma-lee), a Bambara name that the Gullah-Geechee gave to boys.[13] The Bambara people live primarily in Mali, Guinea, Burkina Faso, and Senegal. Molly's name might easily have been what the Gullah-Geechee call basket names, which were often African names given after birth when infants would be laid in baskets to rest or sleep. Basket names were not used for official purposes but by friends and family.

Molly's sister, Hagar, had a biblical name that is Hebrew in origin as well. Historian Charles Joyner wrote that when plantation owners recorded the name Hagar in their records, it was most likely Haga, a Bambara name from Mali.[14]

Molly's mother's name was recorded as Venus on archival records. Joyner explains that the name, Venus, among the enslaved was likely the closest English pronunciation of Bina, Bhina, or Venice, which derived from Aminaba, a name found in Ghana.[15] And Turner identified Bina (pronounced "Beena") as a name given to both boys and girls among the Bambara.[16] Molly's mother's name was identified as Venus, according to documents Molly filed with the US Bureau of Pensions to claim her widow's pension after Sancho died. But Adam Jenkins spelled it Benis in one of the statements in his pension file.

Sancho had a sister named Kitty, according to his Freedmen's Bank Records. Kitty is a name the English and Irish used as a diminutive of Katherine. Yet Turner identified Kiti as also a Gullah-Geechee name given to girls and a word used in the languages in Bambara, Ewe, Twi, and the Kikongo.[17] My great-grandmother's name was Sarah, but Sara is also a name among the Yoruba and Hausa of Nigeria.[18]

To understand my Gullah-Geechee family roots, I also turned to genealogical research to see what my African DNA might reveal. According to AncestryDNA®, 28 percent of my DNA is prevalent in Cameroon-Congo and the Southern Bantu region, which includes Angola, Cameroon, Democratic Republic of the Congo, Equatorial Guinea, Gabon, Namibia, Republic of the Congo, and Zambia; 24 percent seems to come from Nigeria, a region that includes the Central African Republic. Another 4 percent is from Benin and Togo; 3 percent from Mali, Sierra Leone, and Burkina Faso; 3 percent is from Senegal, Guinea, Guinea-Bissau, and Gambia; and 1 percent from Botswana, Lesotho, Malawi, Mozambique, South Africa, and Swaziland.

Another genetic testing service 23andMe found very similar results, but Senegal, Guinea and Guinea-Bissau accounted for 6.6 percent, and the amount estimated from Ghana, Liberia and Sierra Leone was 5.5 percent.

My DNA profile, according to AncestryDNA, is similar to that of other African Americans with ancestors in South Carolina, Georgia, and Virginia, in that it shows origins in a wide swath of West and Central Africa that aligns with the locations from which ships carried enslaved Africans. That analysis confirmed what I suspected. But the lack of specificity in ancestral origins connected to specific ethnic groups and cultures raised that nagging sense, again, of the void I feel. I learned that DNA analysis examines genetic markers that are tied to family lineages, not ethnicities, and pinpoints where those markers are most concentrated. Families move and inter-marry over thousands of years and the fact that some markers are more prevalent in a specific region of a country or continent doesn't mean that your ancestors came from that region; it means only that the likelihood is greater because the markers are more common there than elsewhere.

I turned to African Ancestry, a company that specializes in an-alyzing maternal and paternal DNA for a preponderance of genetic markers that link an ancestor from 500 to 2,000 years in the past to a specific group. My profile linked my maternal DNA to two West African ethnic groups that are known by two names, the Balanta or Brassa people, and the Brame or Macanya people. Both are from the Senegambia region of Africa, Guinea-Bissau, the Gambia, and Senegal.

Although I have found little about the Brame or Macanya, the Balanta were in the Upper Guinea Coast when the Susu were active in the slave trade. The Balanta were among the groups the Portuguese considered "primitive," along with the Djolas, Banhuns, Casangas, Papels, Bjagos, and Bulloms.[19] The Balanta were among the oldest groups in the region and known to be among the best farmers, in the 1500s and 1600s, herding cattle and goats and providing food that neighboring ethnic groups purchased and ate.[20]

The Balanta didn't have a hierarchical society with kings and a class of nobles and class-based social stratification, and they were less involved in the slave trade. The groups with kings and nobility formed alliances with Europeans and targeted the more vulnerable lower classes for enslavement and enslaved rival groups through raids and warfare.[21]

In differentiating the way the Balanta functioned, Rodney wrote: "The Balantas are all small landowners, working their lands on the principle of voluntary reciprocal labor. Thus, when the Balantas clear new areas of swamp for rice cultivation, each one of the working force benefits by receiving a portion of the land reclaimed."[22] The Balantas refused to sell to Europeans and were not seeking to profit off the slave trade. The fact that they avoided trade with those Europeans who colonized the land that became Guinea-Bissau and operated in an egalitarian manner is admirable. But they were not free of all involvement in enslavement although they tried to avoid it. "It is also true that the Balantas and the Djolas remained largely indifferent to the slave trade; and, when raided, retaliated with great ferocity. But, to a greater or lesser extent, all were involved, and all were consumed."[23]

As an African American with roots in this country dating back at least some 200 years, I suspect that some of my ancestors were probably members of stateless societies and more likely victims of the slave trade. But some were probably members of large kingdoms, hierarchical societies, where preying on those without wealth and other ethnic groups was common.

One living African relative, according to AncestryDNA, is a 5th-8th cousin whose ancestry is 100 percent associated with Nigeria, her profile indicates. This distant cousin has an Igbo name. Some 30 million people mostly living in Nigeria are Igbo. Another 5th-8th cousin is Yoruba. When I reached out to her about whether any of her ancestors may have been enslaved during the transatlantic slave trade, she said she wasn't aware of any. The Yoruba and Igbo are both among the largest ethnic groups from Nigeria that were heavily involved in the slave trade with elites in both societies seeking profit from the trade in bodies of the less privileged.

In my experience as an African American, this history of how we ended up here and the roles played by those involved in the translantic slave trade is little discussed. I think about the level of culpability, but, of course, any ancestor who was enslaved and brought to the United States was a clear victim of the trade. Yet, on both sides of the Atlantic the legacy of the slave trade haunts those alive today.

The scars are still present, internally, affecting our consciousness and identity for those of us with ancestors whose identities, family and cultural connectedness were severed.

One might ask why an examination of one's ancestral past matters so much. Why, if African Americans have been in the United States for hundreds of years and have developed a culture from an amalgam of West and Central African ethnicities along with European and Native Americans influences, is such inquiry meaningful?

But the violent severance from our heritage and lineage, coupled with the erasure of our history and marginalization of our past make such research and analysis necessary. Michelle D. Commander, deputy director of the National Museum of African American History and Culture, has written about African Americans' desires to connect with Africa physically through travel and psychically through myth, religion, and folklore. Much of this desire, she argues, comes from what she calls the dispossession caused by the slave trade that is reinforced by ongoing white supremacy and racism.[24] Commander examined this call or pull for connections with Africa across centuries not only in the United States but also in Brazil and other nations with Black people who had a history of enslavement.

"Natal alienation," a term coined by Harvard University sociologist Orlando Patterson, describes the dispossession or psychological trauma that happens when a people are separated from their heritage, land, ancestors, origin stories, myths, religion, language, and culture. Natal alienation, like dispossession, names the painful experience that Black descendants of enslavement and other oppressed people feel.

I have long felt a need to fill the void created by natal alienation and dispossession. Through this research I hope to cure the loss of historical and cultural memory and ethnic connections that were ripped from African Americans through enslavement. Questions about my ancestral origins continue and will never fully be answered. But the connection to my Gullah-Geechee ancestry feels the most complete and the most tangible. On the one hand I've learned of the ancestors who survived a dehumanizing cotton plantation and established a life as freedpeople, participating in an African-derived culture of resilience. While I learned something about their lives in enslavement, much more was revealed when liberation happened.

CHAPTER 4

The Battle for Emancipation

When Confederates fired on Fort Sumter in Charleston, SC, on April 12, 1861, at the start of the Civil War, there were twenty-four plantations on Hilton Head—all focused on growing Sea Island cotton.[1] Eighty-three percent of the population of the Sea Islands was enslaved at the time.[2]

But the life of toil and degradation for Hilton Head's enslaved would change dramatically seven months into the war during the Battle of Port Royal.

The Battle of Port Royal on November 7, 1861, began when Capt. Samuel DuPont decided to attack Confederate troops along Port Royal Sound because of its deep-water harbor. This attack would enable Union naval ships to enforce a blockade that Abraham Lincoln ordered to cut off trade between the Confederacy and Europe. Blockading ports in Wilmington, Savannah, and Charleston was essential to limiting their ability to finance the war.[3]

Thomas Fenwick Drayton, who managed Fish Haul Plantation, was in charge of defending Port Royal Sound from Union attack. Drayton was also president of the Charleston and Savannah Railroad and a brigadier general for the Confederacy. Fort Walker, which Drayton used to fend off the attack, was no match for the fleet of Union ships that began reigning fire on the forts on the day of the battle.[4] Captain Samuel Dupont had fourteen naval vessels involved in the battle moving in an elliptical pattern through two miles of Port Royal Sound's waters as they fired at Fort Walker. The cannon fire from Fort Walker and Fort Beauregard didn't have the power to reach the Union's naval ships. The enslaved on Fish Haul would have been able to see the ships firing since the plantation bordered Port Royal Sound.

When the battle ended some 12,000 Union troops landed on Hilton Head, which would be the site of a large army operation for the Union for several years. Drayton's plantation house would serve as a headquarters for the Department of the South that oversaw the transport of supplies and services for some 40,000 military and civilian personnel.[5]

I can only imagine the excitement my enslaved ancestors must have felt when the battle ended, and the beginnings of liberation took shape. Yet at the same time, the joy might have been mixed with

A photo of the homes of the formerly enslaved on Fish Haul Plantation during the Civil War, shortly after the Battle of Port Royal. Photo by Henry P. Moore. Library of Congress, Prints and Photographs Division.

anxiety because their status as freedpeople was unsettled, as was the war's outcome.

In a 2011 *New York Times* article, Michael Shapiro described the impact on the enslaved: "For the slaves who lived on Port Royal, it was their first step toward freedom. Their owners had fled when Union forces attacked the forts, and most of the slaves either refused to join their owners or were not invited to flee in the first place. Their legal status, however, was not immediately clear: President Lincoln was not prepared to emancipate them, because he did not want to anger the leaders of the slave states that had remained loyal to the Union."[6]

I don't know that accounts exist of how the enslaved on Hiton Head responded during the battle. But in the 1930s, Sam Mitchell gave an account for the Federal Writers Project of how he responded while enslaved at Woodlawn Plantation on Lady's Island, some forty miles from Hilton Head:

> Dat Wednesday in November w'en gun fust shoot to Bay Pin [Point] I t'ought it been t'under rolling, but day ain't no cloud. My mother say, 'Son, dat ain't no t'under, dat Yankee come to gib you Freedom.' I been so glad, I jump up and down and run. My father been splitting rail and Maussa come from Beaufort in de carriage and tear by him yelling for de driver. He told de driver to git his eight-oar boat name Tarrify and carry him to Charleston. My father he run to his house and tell my mother what Maussa say. My mother say, 'You ain't gonna row no boat to Charleston, you go out dat back door and keep agoing.' So my father he did so. Wen dey git nuf [n-er] to row boat and Maussa and his family go right away to Charleston. After Freedom come everybody do as he please.[7]

Seventeen months after the battle, Sancho and my second great-grandmother Molly's twin brothers, Adam and Jacob Jenkins, would have a chance to join the fight for freedom. Some 10,000 of the formerly enslaved were in the region without enslavers. National attention would be focused on Port Royal during the Union Army occupation as abolitionists and missionaries opposed to enslavement moved to the region to support the newly freed by establishing South Carolina's first Black schools, advocating for paid wages for the newly freed and the recruitment of Black soldiers.[8]

The abolitionists and missionaries involved in the Port Royal Experiment saw their efforts as an opportunity to show the ability of the newly freed to live independently and prove that the four million African Americans in the Nation were fit for the possibility of citizenship if the Union won.[9]

But in the first years of the war, as Kevin Dougherty points out, the question of whether the enslaved would be freed would continue to leave uncertainty. Lincoln was reluctant to give any inkling that he would deprive plantation owners of the enslaved because he was concerned that four states where slavery was still legal that had not joined the Confederacy might secede and make the war more difficult. The Gullah-Geechee in the Sea Islands were in limbo in 1861, classified as "contraband" property that had been abandoned and could be seized by the federal government. The concept of "contrabands" originated several months before the battle of Port Royal when Major General Benjamin Butler and Union forces were enforcing the blockade in Hampton Roads, Virginia. Butler declared escaped slaves to be "contraband of war" when they flocked to Union lines, refusing to return them to their enslavers because he knew the enslaved had been used to build forts for Confederate forces.[10]

In May 1861, Union forces began enforcing a blockade of Hampton Roads in the area of Fort Monroe in Hampton, Virginia. In making that declaration, Butler relied on international law and that same classification was applied six months later to enslaved people in the Port Royal area, including Hilton Head. Lincoln's lack of clarity on the status of the enslaved became clear in August 1861 when

Union Army General John Freemont issued a military order freeing them in areas under Union control in Missouri and Lincoln reversed the order.[11]

The issues surrounding how the enslaved would live and the level of control they would have of their labor was contentious during the time, with disagreement among federal officials. Frederick Law Olmsted, a former journalist and opponent of slavery, who was serving as the executive secretary of the US Sanitary Commission (which later became the Red Cross), worked to draft a bill intended to protect former slaves behind Union lines, from disease and hunger. The bill also appointed a board of commissioners to take legal possession of plantations in bankruptcy and to continue their operation through the sale of cotton.[12]

Treasury Secretary Salmon P. Chase, who also opposed slavery, was tasked with proposing a policy for the care of the enslaved. Chase, a radical Republican, one of a group of Republicans who called for the immediate end of slavery, appointed Edward Pierce, a lawyer and abolitionist, to help prepare freed men and women to lead self-sufficient lives when enslavement ended. Chase requested that Pierce develop a plan as Superintendent of Sea Island plantations because he knew Pierce would focus on the welfare of the formerly enslaved and be sympathetic and sensitive to their needs.

Once Pierce arrived, he objected to the intense pressure Black people in the Sea Islands were facing to cultivate cotton so the proceeds could support the war effort. He described the treatment as a "reign of terror" and insisted that the emphasis should be on assisting those behind Union lines instead of simply pushing them to earn money for the federal government's war effort. At the time Pierce was selected to develop a plan for the care of the "contraband slaves," the formerly enslaved were being required to pick and process cotton to support their education, food, housing, education, and training. But Pierce felt those efforts were overly focused on cotton sales to support the war and fell short of what the newly emancipated needed to live as free men and women. Pierce's plan called for the federal government to dispatch teachers to the Port Royal region to teach writing and arithmetic, a radical departure from just a couple of years earlier when teaching the enslaved to write was illegal. Although Pierce praised the industriousness of Black people on the Sea Islands, he called for missionaries to be sent to support the faith of the newly emancipated and inculcate values of "faithful labor" and "clean and healthful habits." Although clearly well-intentioned, the ideas behind the plan reveal Pierce held demeaning and derogatory views of the newly emancipated. He also asked Chase to appoint superintendents to take charge of the plantations and advised that they be urged to use "paternalistic discipline" in directing their work.[13]

What the Gullah-Geechee in the Sea Islands went through during this period while full emancipation remained in limbo seems deeply dehumanizing. First, there was the concept of people being contraband, in essence, property abandoned and seized by the federal government. Then, the paternalistic questioning of their ability to live on their own, viewing them as childlike adults in need of paternal discipline. Although the advocacy of some missionaries for access to land ownership would become clear, Black people weren't included in decisions that would have a radical impact on their lives. Ironically, Black women and men were forced to labor for centuries, offer up their agricultural knowhow, grow crops, tend cattle, clear forests, and build palatial mansions and boats. In addition, they had to hunt and fish and serve as carpenters, blacksmiths, and toolmakers and raise both Black and white children. They did everything except reap the profits and benefits.

Yet, the benefits of this time for the formerly enslaved are evident. The island underwent a radical transformation with the presence of thousands of troops and plantation owners' mansions turned into quarters for Union officers. Freedmen would build docks. Military structures, administrative buildings, and hospitals were erected. Housing would be built. And the formerly enslaved would be able to earn money. Many Black people would leave plantations during the tumult of war and come to Hilton Head to make a living.[14]

Pierce brought missionaries and teachers to the Sea Islands, including members of the American Missionary Association, which set up schools in Hilton Head. The missionaries—mainly from New York, Philadelphia, and Boston—were from various religious organizations and became known as the Gideonites.[15] Most of the Gideonites were white men who came from Ivy League institutions like Harvard and Yale; some had graduated from divinity schools. Some were women who had been teachers and were abolitionists.[16]

During this period conflicts erupted between the Department of War and the Treasury Department—the two agencies involved in the response to the Battle of Port Royal. Military officials and federal officials in Washington proposed multiple ideas on how to structure life in the Sea Islands with both sides working to win over the support of the formerly enslaved, seeking validation of their proposals.[17] Military officers resented the Gideonites and were critical of Pierce's mission, thinking that it was overly concerned with the well-being of the formerly enslaved. Some expressed virulent racist attitudes, referring to the Gideonites with racial epithets as "n— lovers." The US Sanitary Commission had the formerly enslaved working on cotton plantations with cotton agents receiving a commission on sales with the bulk going to support expenses on the plantations.[18]

Although they were benevolent and dedicated to the welfare of the newly freed, the Gideonites favored an economic model of "free labor" where the workers would decide where they would work and for whom. The Gideonites believed that northerners had a superior sense of morals and a better economic sense and thought the newly freed should work on plantations that would be managed by white northerners. But the newly freed saw land ownership as a greater means of independence and freedom. They wanted to be free of white domination and a wage-labor system and saw owning and farming their own land as the way to do it.[19]

Although Pierce was appointed by Chase to oversee the plantations, Secretary of War Edwin Stanton appointed Brigadier General Rufus Saxton to seize the plantations in April 1862 and oversee protection and employment of those living on the plantations.[20] The formerly enslaved were living with families in cabins that measured about 12 × 16 feet, and many were in poor condition. Those who fled plantations on the mainland and other islands were living in tents or in wooden barracks, with each room housing between five and fifteen people. Food, clothing, and medical care were sorely lacking. Some had little or no clothes and poor diets.[21]

In October, Major General Orsby M. Mitchel, who led the Department of the South, which was based on Hilton Head, decided to build a town on Drayton Plantation for the newly freed near the military camp along the banks of Port Royal Sound. Part of Fish Haul was used as a campground for the First South Carolina Volunteers, which was the first Black regiment formed by the Union.[22] Mitchel sought to improve the quality of life for those living in the barracks in poor conditions. He devised a plan for a freepeople's town that would incorporate streets, quarter-acre lots, and a town government with a mayor, treasurer, appointed by the military commander, and a town council, town supervisor, recorder, and marshall elected by Black residents. All children ages 6 to 15 would be required to attend a public school and taxes would be collected.[23] The town of Mitchelville was built on 200 acres of plantation land that wasn't being cultivated.[24]

In recent years, a nonprofit organization, Historical Mitchelville Freedom Park, formed to preserve the history of Mitchelville, establishing a park on the site where the town existed. I talked with the organization's executive director, Ahmand Ward, about the significance of this town to African American history. In his view, "Mitchelville is not only notable because it was the first freedmen's town that was created for African Americans. But it was built by and run by African Americans. They built homes on quarter-acre lots, a praise house, and a school. They established a set of laws. They built their own homes and competed with the military to see which model design would be most suitable and the newly freed won."[25]

What's particularly notable, according to Ward, is the agency Black people demonstrated in the transition to freedom. "They went from being property to owning property," said Ward, noting that they no longer had to wear rags and slave cloth—the cheap, coarse cotton clothes, also called Negro cloth—that was manufactured for the enslaved. But they began making their own clothes and adorning themselves. Archaeological digs turned up evidence of beads and jewels in places where the newly emancipated lived.

Just months before Mitchelville was established in April 1862, a *New York Times* reporter covered a meeting in the "negro quarters" of the Department of the South, the former Drayton Plantation, and noted the jewelry and multicolored African headwraps that Black women, then considered contraband slaves, were wearing:

> All were decently dressed; some of the women indulging in jewelry and hoops that might have excited the admiration of those of pale complexion. The distinguishing feature in their dress was the turban, which is generally worn, and with a good deal of grace, giving to them an oriental and picturesque appearance. These head-dresses are of all colors, from the neutral tint up to the flaming red, and not unfrequently combining half a dozen colors in a plaid.[26]

Several months before Mitchelville was established in April 1862, Major General David Hunter who succeeded Brigadier General Thomas W. Sherman as head of the Department of the South began executing a plan to create a Black regiment. He sought permission from Washington to form Black units and requested 50,000 muskets, ammunition, and 50,000 pairs of pantaloons. Although some military officers began creating Black units in Louisiana, Kansas, and

South Carolina, none had been officially sanctioned. Hunter didn't wait for volunteers or permission from Washington—he ordered commanders to round up able-bodied Black men to serve. Many in the population of newly freed were afraid. Nevertheless, he raised a regiment. However, he disbanded it on August 10, 1862, because Lincoln hadn't exercised the powers he received from Congress that authorized the use of Black troops. Two weeks later on August 25, 1862, Stanton gave Brigadier General Rufus Saxton the power to arm and equip "volunteers of African descent" including providing training, disciplining them and offering equal pay and rations.[27]

Saxton reorganized the First Regiment of South Carolina Volunteers and then the 2nd Regiment on January 13, 1863, just days after Abraham Lincoln issued the Emancipation Proclamation, freeing the enslaved in the states that had rebelled. Hunter then began organizing the 3rd Regiment (later referred to as the 21st Regiment) of the US Colored Troops in April 1863 for the campaign against Charleston. Some of the recruits for the 3rd regiment, who would join Sancho, Adam, and Jacob, were among the enslaved freed during the Combahee River Raid that Harriet Tubman helped lead.[28]

In the raids on June 1–2, 1863, Tubman led hundreds of Black troops from the 2nd regiment, organized on Hilton Head, up the Combahee River to liberate rice plantations and free the enslaved. She did this by working with Black mariners to spy on the locations of Confederate troops. Tubman depended on the knowledge of the mariners to navigate waterways that were mined with explosives. Black troops led the raid. Some 750 enslaved were freed. And no union soldiers were lost.[29]

No record that I can find tells how Sancho, Adam, and Jacob and the other sixty-eight Hilton Head men who were part of the 21st regiment felt about the risk they took by enlisting. Joining an army during a major civil war fought over slavery put them and their families in peril since the man they labored for, who was legally considered their owner, was a Confederate military leader who took up arms to maintain enslavement. If the Union Army wasn't victorious, it's hard to imagine that Brigadier General Thomas Fenwick Drayton, who was in charge of the Confederate forces on Hilton Head, would not have sold all three men away from their families or devised some other severe punishment for having the gall to try and free themselves. They might have even lost their lives. Some of the enslaved in Beaufort County and the Port Royal area who refused to flee with plantation owners when the Union Army attacked were killed.[30]

But Adam, Jacob and Sancho must have wanted liberation badly enough to enlist despite their fears. The 21st regiment was organized for the campaign against Charleston, the primary slave market in the nation where the war started. The incredible wealth built through the brutal rice and cotton plantations would have been visible from the mansions in the city's center to the palatial homes and gardens of the opulent Ashley River plantations, including Drayton Hall, that Thomas Fenwick Drayton's ancestor built. It was in that space, with the weight of that wealth and the worst aspects of the trade and enslavement, that Adam, Jacob, and Sancho served to win freedom.

The 21st Regiment were stationed on Folly Island, Morris Island, and Coles Island from April 1864 to February 1865.[31] Adam, Jacob, and Sancho remained soldiers until they were discharged in 1866. One incident during the war caused twenty members of the regiment to lose their lives. Colonel Eugene Kozlay, commander of the 54th Regiment of New York Volunteers, was summoned to a meeting with a general in James Island and went there by boat with thirty aboard on July 2, 1864. The boat Sancho was riding in capsized at night during high tide as waters began surging.[32]

Kozlay described what happened in his journal:

While in the middle of the Stono River, the gun boat Iris took us in tow, and while turning, the last boat was capsized. I jumped from the boat in order to escape the others. What a sight! What a cry for help cut the air through. It was night. The tide came in very strong. The waves were high. And the poor fellows swept away from the surface of the water. In their last hope, clinging and pulling anything they could find. I was pulled down twice. But God almighty saved me; however, I caught hold of an oar, and on that I kept up myself, until assistance arrived from the Iris, and from about 30 about 10 of us were picked up.[33]

Sancho gave his own account of this accident and the injury he suffered a few decades later in his pension claims to the US Bureau of Pensions: "The boat was towed over by the tug that was taking us. Twenty-one men drowned when the boat turned over. A gun fell between my legs and mashed my right testicle. I fell in the water but caught hold of the boat and was taken on shore."[34]

The end of the battle in Charleston would come six months later, after a 545-day siege of Charleston, the longest in US history. Blain Roberts and Ethan Kytle, who wrote a book covering the war's end in Charleston, described the siege in the *New York Times* as part of the paper's "Disunion" series on February 19, 2015. They discussed how the 21st Regiment entered Charleston as liberators to enforce the Union victory on February 18, 1865. At the time, nearly two dozen fires blazed around the city after retreating Confederate forces set bales of cotton and arms and ammunition on fire to keep Union forces from getting control of them. Members of the 21st would extinguish the fires.[35]

Over the next several days thousands of newly freed Blacks celebrated, cheering the troops, laughing, dancing with joy when they saw them, and praising them. "Charleston was transformed from the birthplace of secession into the graveyard of slavery. In parades, commemorations and demonstrations, local freedmen and women joined with the occupying force to mark Union victory and the end of the peculiar institution," Roberts and Kytle wrote. The well-known Massachusetts 54th regiment and the all-Black 55th regiment were part of the celebration. The ancestors of Sancho, Adam, Jacob, and their fellow soldiers likely were brought to Charleston chained aboard slave ships and sold at the numerous slave markets there. The three must have felt uncontainable joy at helping to be part of slavery's end.

Festivals of freedom continued for months in Charleston in the spring and summer of 1865 as liberated men and women celebrated. The most memorable and largest celebration, according to Roberts and Kytle, may have been the one festival, involving the 21st regiment, held on March 21 on the Citadel Green, the parade ground for the South Carolina Military Academy. This was the place where white men prepared for military careers and defended against insurrection of the enslaved.[36]

According to Yale Historian David Blight, another large celebration of freedom was held on May 1, 1865, and became known as Decoration Day, the precursor to Memorial Day. On May 1, 1865, Blight stated, Black Charleston residents exhumed the bodies of some 257 Union prisoners who had died of disease and were buried in a mass grave at a former racecourse and jockey club. The deceased had been forced to live in squalid conditions while imprisoned. Black residents reinterred the bodies to give them a dignified commemoration, erecting a fence to encircle the burial ground. They built an archway, including the words "Martyrs of the Racecourse." Some 10,000 Black residents, led by school children holding roses, sang John Brown's body and the Union anthem during the procession. Women carried crosses, baskets of flowers, and wreaths. Union soldiers marched as well.[37]

Three years after the first celebrations in Charleston, a group of Union veterans decided to honor the war dead with flowers. A retired union general set May 30 at Arlington National Cemetery for Decoration Day. The commemoration later became Memorial Day and morphed into a celebration of both deceased union and Confederate veterans. Yet the context around Black liberators and formerly enslaved people organizing a commemoration and celebration of freedom decorating graves with flowers was erased from the narrative of the holiday's origins.[38]

Despite the renaming of Decoration Day as Memorial Day, Decoration Day would continue to be celebrated in the Georgia Sea Islands well into the twentieth century to commemorate liberation. Hilton Head residents would travel to Beaufort to celebrate and memorialize deceased Civil War veterans with parades, marching and music played by "jump-up" bands. Celebrations with parties and live bands would start on May 27, two days before Beaufort's Decoration Day festivities.[39]

At the war's end, Mitchelville was thriving, noted Tom Barton in an *Island Packet* article on August 26, 2014. The town had a population of 1,500 people. The residents worked for members of the military as carpenters, blacksmiths, cooks, guides, stable hands, and mechanics earning as much as $12 per month, Barton wrote. Some sold vegetables, eggs, and seafood. Others worked as day laborers on cotton plantations.[40]

Four stores in Mitchelville were permitted by the army and operated by northerners, and they sold fabric, clothes, pots and pans, tea kettles, washboards, rolling pins, fish nets, buttons pomade, thimbles, and eyeglasses.[41] As an all-Black self-governing town run by the formerly enslaved, Mitchelville attracted national press attention.[42] The famous abolitionist, William Lloyd Garrison, visited the town to see how life for the newly freed was progressing. Red Cross founder Clara Barton and Underground railroad leader and abolitionist Harriet Tubman were among those who visited Mitchelville. Tubman, in fact, brought more than 100 recruits for the US Colored Troops to the recruiting office in Hilton Head.[43] Clara Barton lived in Hilton Head in 1863 and organized classes for the newly freed.[44] The transformation that happened within a few years was astounding. Hilton Head became a port through which military supplies would enter to help the union. The population grew to 50,000. Three hotels began operating along with a hospital and a prison and two weekly newspapers.[45]

When the Civil War ended, the national attention on Hilton Head waned. When the military left in 1868, the income Mitchel-ville residents derived from providing services and selling goods evaporated.[46] The town began disintegrating and no longer existed by 1890.

Even before the military left in 1868, it was clear that the vision of Hilton Head's Gullah-Geechee residents was not to reside in a town but to own land, fish, and farm and to live among themselves. And for generations after, they would do just that: build a self-sustaining community with its own spiritual traditions and cultural traditions despite incredible hardship.

CHAPTER 5

The Land That Liberates

❁

In January 1865, when asked what Hilton Head's Black residents would do after the war, Reverend Abraham Murchinson, the pastor of First African Baptist and mayor of Mitchelville, reportedly said, "Go out into the land and make their homes there. Buy 20 acres of land. That is what should be: once settled on his 20 acres, no one can oppress the negro hereafter. But without the land, all the teaching, all the philanthropy, all the Christianity of the world cannot save him from the oppression of his selfish neighbor who holds the means of bread in his own hands."[1]

It's clear that Murchinson, who had escaped slavery, saw land ownership as the means through which liberation and freedom from racial oppression would be achieved. He put forth a clear vision of self-determination and self-preservation through farming. As the pastor of the first church for Gullah-Geechee people, Murchinson was a person of power and influence within the community. His view of the need for land ownership stood in stark contrast to the Gideonites—most of whom thought the Gullah-Geechee should work for wages as a means to develop thrift and independence.

The concept of distributing "40 acres and a mule" to the newly freed was conceived in January 1865 after Union General William Tecumseh Sherman and Secretary of War Ed Stanton met with twenty Black pastors in Savannah, Georgia, thirty miles from Hilton Head. When Sherman asked the men what their goals were for life in freedom, Reverend Garrison Frazier, a spokesman for the group, said: "The way we can best take care of ourselves is to have land and turn it and till it by our own labor—that is, by the labor of the women and children and old men; and we can soon maintain ourselves and have something to spare. And to assist the Government, the young men should enlist in the service of the Government and serve in such manner as they may be wanted. We want to be placed on land until we are able to buy it and make it our own."[2] Fifteen of the pastors had been enslaved. Frazier had been a slave as well and bought his wife's freedom for $1,000 in gold and silver.[3]

When asked whether they wanted to live among white people or in colonies by themselves, Frazier was also clear about the desire to live separately, citing the high level of racial prejudice: "I would prefer to live by ourselves, for there is a prejudice against us in the South that will take years to get over; but I do not know that I can answer for my brethren." Of the twenty pastors questioned, only one disagreed, saying he would prefer to live in integrated communities.[4]

Four days after Sherman's meeting with the pastors, he followed the separatist vision he heard from the pastors and issued Special Field Order No. 15, which set aside land from Charleston to Jacksonville, Florida, and thirty miles inland for exclusive Black settlement, allowing Black people to reside there without being moved.[5]

The order stated:

At Beaufort, Hilton Head, Savannah, Fernandina, St. Augustine, and Jacksonville, the blacks may remain in their chosen or accustomed vocations; but on the islands, and in the settlements hereafter to be established, no white person whatever, unless military officers and soldiers detailed for duty, will be permitted to reside; and the sole and exclusive management of

affairs will be left to the freed people themselves, subject only
to the United States military authority and the acts of Congress.
By the laws of war, and orders of the President of the United
States, the negro is free, and must be dealt with as such.[6]

Sherman's order designated 400,000 acres of land between
Charleston and the St. Johns River in Florida for Black settlement,
scholar Henry Louis Gates wrote in an article posted by PBS.[7]

Gates saw the massive land redistribution for African Americans, created by the order, as an unprecedented step by the federal government and a significant attempt at reparations in a large
portion of the South. "The promise was the first systemic attempt
to provide a form of reparations to newly freed slaves, and it was
astonishingly radical for its time," Gates wrote. "What most of us
haven't heard is that the idea really was generated by Black leaders
themselves."

Unlike so much of the Black freedom struggle that focused on
racial integration, the pastors who met with Stanton and Sherman, like Murchinson, sought voluntary separation as the best
solution for racial oppression and independence. Under the order,
Black people could govern themselves, and white people would
be excluded from the area unless they were members of the military. Lives began changing immediately after the order. One of the
ministers who met with Sherman moved immediately with 1,000
freedmen and women to Skidaway Island, Georgia, to establish a
community where he served as governor. And some 40,000 of the
formerly enslaved settled on 400,000 acres by June, six months after
the field order was issued, according to Gates.

The Freedmen's Bureau, shorthand for The Bureau of Refugees,
Freedmen and Abandoned Lands, was an agency created in 1865
through congressional legislation to assist many of the millions of
newly freed, particularly around education and health care. The
federal government spent more than $5 million on day and night

schools, industrial schools, Sunday schools, and colleges from 1865 to 1871. Most historically Black colleges and universities received support from the Freedmen's Bureau. Forty-six hospitals were set up in fourteen states with more than 5,000 beds.[8]

But part of the Freedmen's Bureau charge was to redistribute 800,000 acres of plantation land, seized for nonpayment of taxes, allowing it to be leased and eventually sold to Black farmers. After Lincoln was assassinated, President Andrew Johnson restored the ownership rights for plantation owners whose land was seized during the war. It could be returned if they received a pardon and paid their back taxes. The law made an exception for land seized in the Port Royal area. Although most land was restored between 1865 and 1868, tens of thousands of Black farmers in the Deep South were able to buy the seized land. In South Carolina, about 33,000 plantations were sold to 93,000 small farmers both Black and White.[9]

The Freedman's Savings Bank gave loans to the newly freed to encourage economic development. Sancho opened a bank account there. A copy of a bank record from that year lists Sancho's age as 25, his complexion as "Black" and his occupation as "farmer." From that document, I learned the names of Sancho's family members, also formerly enslaved: his mother, Heena; his brothers, Paris and Murray; and his sisters, Kitty and Nancy. Sancho's opening of a Freedmen's Bank account is a likely indication of his intent to save money to buy land.[10]

The Gullah-Geechee in the Sea Islands were able to begin buying seized plantation land in 1863 before Sherman's order was issued in 1865, but they had to compete for land ownership with northern capitalists who sought to buy large tracts of former plantation land and profit from hiring the newly freed as laborers. Union Army General Rufus Saxton advocated successfully for some of the seized land to be set aside for the military and charitable purposes because he feared it would all go to northern speculators. He was able to amend a tax law that allowed for the forfeited land to be auctioned off and pause the sales process. Of 80,000 acres seized, only 21,000 acres were sold before the pause. Some 2,000 acres were bought by the newly freed.[11]

Gideonite Edward Philbrick, who had been a member of the Massachusetts Anti-Slavery Society, and a friend of William Lloyd Garrison was able to buy eleven former plantations and lease two others, controlling 7,000 acres of land. His goal as a free-market capitalist was to make money from cotton sales through cheap labor. He believed that former plantations managed by northerners would have moral and financial benefits for them.[12]

But the newly freed had a strong ally in Saxton who advocated vigorously for federal land policies to foster Black land ownership. He made it clear that wealthy white northerners could lock Black people out of land ownership and thus called on Lincoln to give them an advantage in their ability to purchase land.[13]

While Gideonites were managing cotton plantations and the growing of other crops for Philbrick, Lincoln agreed to new land sales in late 1863. Some 16,000 acres out of 40,000 were designated for sale to members of the "African Race" at $1.25 an acre. Saxton spread the word to African Americans interested in land that they should put down cash deposits at his office and 160 did so within 10 days of Lincoln's order. If a Black person put a downpayment on a parcel of land, it would prevent anyone else from bidding on that land, according to Lincoln's order. By the end of January, 6,000 acres had been sold to African Americans.[14]

Scholars have discussed how the competing interests, ideas, and visions among white northerners enabled the newly freed to own land in different ways over time. Between 1862 and 1865, the newly freed were able to acquire land through rent-to-own programs and auction sales on former plantation land in Port Royal Island, St. Helena, and Lady's Island (also in Beaufort County). Saxton had encouraged freedpeople to settle in houses on former plantation land because of a preemption that required land purchasers to live in the area of the land they sought for at least six months. Sales and land division records show a ten-acre grid pattern throughout St. Helena Island.[15]

It appears that my great-great uncle Adam Jenkins was able to buy 15 acres of land in Port Royal Island in 1866, consisting of a 5-acre and 10-acre parcel as a result of the land seizures. Port Royal Island, like Hilton Head, is in Beaufort County. The certificates state that the sale was authorized through an act of Congress allowing for tax collection in insurrectionary districts through the bureau organized for the relief of freedmen and refugees.[16]

When Johnson overturned Sherman's order allowing land redistribution to the newly freed, it enabled former plantation owners throughout the South to reclaim land. But in the Sea Islands in the Beaufort area, the government-maintained possession of much of the land, and it allowed the Gullah-Geechee to own substantial portions, solidifying their ability to form communities. As Brabec and Richardson explained, "In spite of the government's contradictory and changing policies, by 1870 much of the islands were owned by a society of free Black farmers who had an opportunity to become self-sufficient."[17]

Despite the progress in land ownership, the departure of the military from Hilton Head hampered the ability of freedpeople to earn wages through services and sales to military officers and soldiers. "Money and Northern support for the freedmen quickly dried up after the war, leaving most blacks with little beyond their small plots of land (obtained from the previous slave plantations) which they carefully guarded, for 'they well understood the basis of their security,'" the author of an archaeological survey of a portion of the former Fish Haul Plantation wrote.[18]

Researchers in another study said: "The Headquarters of the Department of the South moved to Charleston upon the war's end and Federal occupation in 1865. Hilton Head Island was no longer necessary as a base of operations. The federal military force was gradually reduced and the town's businesses closed."[19] The abandoned shops, post offices, hospital, and customs house became remnants, artifacts of a war-time economy, and because they no longer served a purpose, residents stripped wood and beams to build their houses. When the military was there, a school for the newly freed was operating in half of the former mansion where Thomas Fenwick Drayton lived with his wife Emma Catherine Pope. The last of the schools run by missionaries closed in 1870. A few years earlier, one of the teachers lamented the dwindling number of students and how the return to an agrarian economy required school-age children to help their parents on small farms. She spoke of the lack of jobs and people living on hominy and fish or soup with little income.[20]

Sancho and other freedpeople would begin owning parcels of Fish Haul Plantation a decade after the Civil War when the Drayton family decided to reclaim the land, pay off back taxes, and sell it. Since the end of the Civil War, large parts of the plantation were being rented by Gullah-Geechee residents of Hilton Head and crops grown on the farm would help pay rental costs. Bacchus Singleton rented it in 1865, 1866, and 1867 for $220. And Summer Christopher, who had been enslaved there and knew Adam Jenkins when he was enslaved, rented it in 1868 for $90. But in early 1874, the Drayton family began seeking to reclaim Fish Haul because of a law that allowed former plantation owners to redeem title to land the federal government had seized. In 1875, the Drayton and Pope heirs reclaimed ownership of 1,300 for $407 in back taxes and interests and began dividing and selling off portions in 1876 to people who were formerly enslaved.[21] Sancho, James Washington, and Phillis were among the early buyers acquiring sixteen acres on January 22, 1877.[22]

Gabriel Gardner, who bought the largest parcel (650 acres) of Fish Haul land from the Draytons in 1885, sold it to ten people who partitioned it among themselves in 1894. Among the ten were Adam Jenkins who gained title to 79 acres. James Grant, Simon Grant, Dennis Smith, Minus Chisolm, and Ansel and Phillis Holmes each received title to 79 acres as well. Summer Christopher received 69 acres and E. and S. Gardner received 61 acres. Perry Holmes received one 23-acre tract and one 56-acre tract. Richard "Pompey" Smalls received two tracts of 23 acres and a tract of 56 acres of land.[23] Minus Chisolm and James Grant had been enslaved along with Adam on this same land.[24]

According to Heritage Library researchers, the majority of Hilton Head's plantation owners (unlike the Draytons) did not seek restitution of their property rights by paying back taxes and seeking a presidential pardon. Sea Island cotton was no longer as valuable, there was no free labor, and their livestock, farm tools and barns were gone. The federal government sold substantial portions off and prices were sometimes as little as 1/20th of what the land was worth before the war.[25]

This process of buying former plantation land from the federal government enabled the formation of an intact community. "Bit by bit, parcel by parcel, freedmen scraped and sacrificed to buy a few acres of land whenever they could. A few would manage to buy large land tracts . . . The men and women freed from slavery shaped what came next on Hilton Head for generations to come: tiling the land and harvesting fish and shellfish form the sea; forming close family and community ties: living in small settlements scattered across the island near former plantation sites; observing church laws; and holding to old African customs."[26]

Throughout the island, families clustered homes together in kinship-based compounds. "Nuclear families occupied single homes, which were then clustered in groups of extended families. "Extended families" refer to kinship networks created by blood as well as place; it was, for instance, not uncommon for families to further organize themselves according to the plantations from which they had fled. Through the compact clustering of the Mitchelville houses, kinship networks that had been severed under slavery were then reaffirmed, rediscovered, and renewed."[27]

By 1880, about 2,500 lived on Hilton Head—some 98 percent of them Black. By 1900, the several hundred Gullah-Geechee families owned one-quarter of the 12 × 5-mile island.[28] An index of Hilton Head's deeds compiled by Heritage Library researchers after the Civil War shows transfers of land from the following former plantations: Brick Yard (Shipyard), Grasslawn, Sand Hill, Cotton Hope, Marshland, Chaplins, Gardner, Spanish Wells, Fairfield, Honey Horn, Stoney, Seabrook, Lawton, Fairfield, Cherry Hill, Muddy Creek, Otter Hole and Jarvis Creek, and Piney Woods.[29]

As African Americans migrated north, the population of Hilton Head would shrink. Between 1870 and 1880, the number of households dropped from 776 to 678. By 1910, it was down to 507 households. Between 1880 and 1910, the population decreased from 2,500 to 2,068 residents. And the dwindling would continue to roughly 300 in 1930.[30]

More people were leaving than staying. The population that existed in the post–Civil War decades had dramatically decreased. The land, the primary resources that sustained the Gullah-Geechee, was not getting more valuable. People were still living without indoor plumbing, telephones, paved roads or electricity.[31]

However, something about the island, the community, the land, the independence and freedom must have kept them believing in its value. Many worked in Savannah at times but returned to the land. Despite the difficulties, hundreds of Gullah-Geechee families held onto their land and farmed well into the twentieth century.

CHAPTER 6

The Ancestors Find Their Way

I cannot ask my great-great-grandfather what his life was like when he was defined as chattel and confined to a cotton plantation, laboring in stifling heat where yellow fever and malaria snatched lives. If I could talk with him, I'd ask how he managed to survive the horrors of enslavement. I'd want to know what his daily life was like as a member of the US Colored Troops. And what he felt and did when he realized enslavement was over and he'd be freed. And I'd want to understand why he decided to return to the Gullah-Geechee community on Hilton Head when he worked so many jobs in Savannah, where financially at least, life might have been easier.

My Second Great-Grandfather, Sancho Christopher

I only had a few bits of information about my second great-grandfather, Sancho Christopher, all passed down orally: I heard he liked to be called Sancho, which was his given name. Aunt Aggie, who first told me about the name Sancho, said he did not like to be called Samuel, the name introduced when he registered for the US Colored Infantry. The name Samuel stuck with him on some official records for the rest of his life, with his given name,

Sancho—sometimes spelled Sanco—listed as an alternate name. At times Sancho was recorded as his surname with Christopher as his first name.

Although the details passed down orally are scant, Sancho left a record about his life through multiple depositions as he sought disability pension benefits and pension increases that were available to Civil War veterans. Those records housed at the US National Archives and Records Administration contain some details of the war, his injury and illnesses, what he did after the war, and the names of soldiers he served with, some of whom were enslaved on the same plantation. Agricultural census documents indicate what he farmed and how much land he owned.

In a deposition given in 1901, Sancho named his enslaver: "I was born here on Hilton Head, S.C., April 15, 1843. I was born a slave to R.P. Pope who lived where I was born." (Heritage Library researchers think it likely that Sancho was referring to R.R. Pope, Richard Richardson Pope, who was born at Fish Haul in 1817.) Sancho then names his father, Prince G. Christopher. "Prince G. Christopher was my father and his master was mine. I don't know how he got his name; when a slave I was called Sanco, but when enlisted I was called Samuel."[1]

It seems apparent from his statement that the person who enlisted him must have misunderstood the pronunciation of his name and thought it was Samuel. Or the person decided to give him a conventional American name instead of the unfamiliar African name. As a formerly enslaved man who was newly emancipated, it's possible his personhood was not even recognized, so trying to figure out how to spell the name might not have even occurred to them.

It seems that Sancho knew little about his father's lineage; he didn't know where the name Christopher came from. A pre–Civil War record shows that Sancho's life was assigned a dollar value. The property inventory from Mary B. Pope's 1857 will contain a list of fifty-three enslaved people on Fish Haul Plantation. Sancho

Sancho mentions his enslaver and his father's enslaver in this 1901 deposition for his disability pension application.

had been enslaved by the Pope family, but Fish Haul's ownership was associated with Thomas Fenwick Drayton before the Civil War because of his marriage to Mary Pope's daughter, Emma Catherine Pope. Drayton was managing the plantation in trust for his children.[2]

Drayton described the inventory as the "goods, chattels and personal estate of Mary B. Pope." Below that it reads: Numbers of Negroes listed. Sancho was considered a top dollar Negro. He was 14 years old. His life was assessed a value of $1,000. I assume that was based on the profits his body could produce. Only a few others in the list of fifty-three were considered to be worth as much.

Five years later, the Battle of Port Royal would end that life of enslavement. And nineteen months later at about age 20, he'd volunteer for the US Colored Infantry and serve for three years. Sancho would continue the transformation from a human-being considered property who could be bought, sold, traded, given away as a wedding gift, or willed to an heir to a man in full possession of his own body, making his own life choices as a freed man. Liberation meant he could get legally married to my great-great-grandmother Molly. The two got married eight months after Sancho was discharged from the army, right before New Year's Eve.

"On December 30, 1866 I married Margaret Jenkins here at Hilton Head; Rev. Murchinson of the Baptist Church married us," he said, according to the deposition.[3]

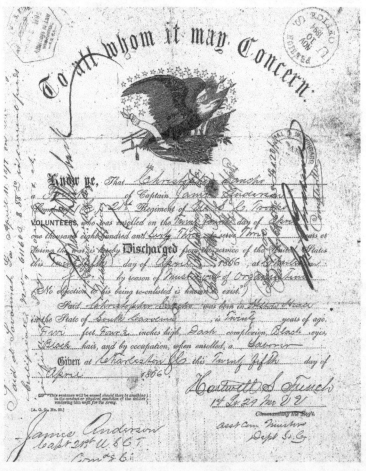

Sancho's discharge papers from the US Colored Infantry after three years of service.

Murchinson performed many marriage ceremonies when the Civil War ended. "There was an explosion of marriages on Hilton Head Island at First African Baptist Church, the only Gullah church on the island at the time," Barnwell, Grant and Campbell wrote.[4] Unlike marriages among the enslaved, Sancho and Molly could give their union the dignity that comes with a legally recognized marriage. And Sancho didn't have to deal with the paternalistic practice of having to ask his enslaver for permission to marry who he wanted. In addition to getting married, being freed allowed him to buy land, farm and work various jobs in Savannah, and raise his daughter, Sarah, with Molly.

Sancho must have been saving money. Records from the Freedman's Savings and Trust Company, known as the Freedman's Bank, show he opened an account in 1865. The Freedman's Bank was designed to help freedmen and freedwomen save their money and build a future. In his bank records, Sancho listed the names of his immediate family: his parents, Prince and Heena; his four siblings, Paris, Murray, Kitty, and Nancy; and my great-great-grandmother, listed by her given name, Margaret. The form states he was 25 years old at the time. Sancho indicated he was a farmer living in Hilton Head, where he was born and raised.[5]

In 1868, Sancho gained access to political power for the first time by registering to vote. He joined more than 1,000 residents of Hilton Head and Bluffton in exercising his citizenship rights.[6] The Agricultural Census of 1868 lists an S. Christopher, with 7.5 acres of land in cultivation and 3 acres planted. S. Christopher produced 150 pounds of long-staple cotton, 5 bushels of rice from 0.5 acres of land, 30 bushels of corn from 3 acres of land and 25 bushels of sweet potatoes from 1 acre of land. One swine was listed. S. Christopher's farm tools were valued at $500.[7] What's unclear is whether this listing in the census applied to Sancho or Summer Christopher, who had also been enslaved at Fish Haul. What S. Christopher grew seemed typical of what hundreds of Gullah-Geechee grew on subsistence farms in Hilton Head. Most, like S. Christopher, Adam, and Jacob, had a hog. Some more prosperous Gullah-Geechee farmers owned a few donkeys, horses, or cows, the agricultural census showed.

In choosing to own land, like many other Black families from Hilton Head that served with him before the war, Sancho chose the independence and safety of the Gullah-Geechee community and lack of daily visible white domination and discrimination. But he also sought to earn income or prosper financially, given the twenty years he spent working in Savannah while holding on to farmland. For the two decades of his life from 1893 to 1914, he lived on Hilton Head on the farm. Sancho would have been among the first generation in liberation to split his time between the Gullah-Geechee farm life and labor jobs in Savannah. "I had lived in Savannah from 1873 to 1893; I lived all over the city and the rest of the time I lived here on Hilton Head," he stated in the 1901 deposition.[8]

He seems to have learned to read and write within a few years of discharge. Sancho's Freedman's Bank account record shows he indicated he was the owner of the bank account with an "X." And Christopher Sancho was written above and around the "X" in cursive. But by the 1870 census, Sancho, whose name seems to have been misspelled as Simco, indicated he could read and write and was a farmer. Molly indicated she could read but couldn't write. By the 1870 census, Sancho and Molly were raising a 5-year-old girl, Isabella. A few years later in 1874 Molly gave birth to my great-grandmother Sarah. Sarah doesn't show up until the 1880 census when she was 6 under her nickname Pink. Sarah would tell my mother many decades later that she was the only one of six children that Sancho and Molly had who survived.[9]

In a statement for his pension, Sancho listed the streets in Savannah he lived on: Bay Street, Montgomery Street, Farm Street, William Street, Price Street, Broughton Street, Little James Street, West Boundary Street, and Indian Street. Sancho indicated that he moved frequently because of financial troubles.[10]

His health conditions, the war injury to his groin, and failing eyesight seemed to make steady employment difficult. Sancho said: "I worked where I could get it." At one point he worked at Habersham's rice mill in Savannah. James Habersham operated a major commercial business in colonial Georgia in the 1740s and once owned 15,000 acres of land and had 200 enslaved people working on his rice plantations.[11]

Sancho bought land from the Drayton family during the twenty years that he worked in Savannah. It seems that he could've abandoned Hilton Head permanently and stayed there. But land ownership in the island of his birth clearly mattered. Sancho's physical maladies and disabilities from the war seemed to mount in the last few decades of his life, and he sought increases in his pension. In a pension bureau document from 1893, Sancho's disabilities are listed as rupture, piles, rheumatism, almost totally blind, chronic articular rheumatism, lumbago, and disease of the throat. In 1906, in the last decade of his life, Sancho was described as having rheumatism, piles, diseased throat and eyes, heart and chest pains, vertigo, poor teeth, senile disability, and a kidney and lung condition.[12]

In 1910, according to federal census records, Sancho (listed as Samuel) was living in a multigenerational household with his wife Margaret (Molly), their daughter Sarah, and four of her children (my great-aunts and uncles): Aggie, Clarence, Julia, and Benjamin. Sancho pressed his claim for pension increases over some twenty years, his pension file shows. His persistence in applying, which required medical examinations and depositions from witnesses, paid off. In 1883, he began receiving a $6 per month veterans' pension. The pension was increased to $8 a month in 1904, $12 in 1907, $19 in 1912, and $25 for the last year of his life.[13] In that last year, $25 was equivalent to $600 per month in 2020. Sancho died on October 30, 1914, when he was about 71 years old.[14]

The story passed down in the family from my great-grandmother to my mother is that Sancho required her, his only daughter, Sarah, to marry Moses Polite, his best friend. Sarah lived with my mother and grandmother throughout my mother's childhood. And my mother remembers Sarah saying that her father "made her marry an old man." She told my mother she "had her own person whom she wanted to marry," but her father made her marry Moses. And while she didn't love Moses at first, she told my mother she grew to love him. In many West African cultures, parents arrange marriages and play a major role in selecting their child's spouse. Traditionally, romantic love wasn't considered a good enough reason for matrimony. Whether Sancho was following an African tradition of arranged marriages or not, he didn't recognize Sarah's desire to make her own marital choices. And he operated out of a patriarchy that disempowered her and bothered her enough that she told my mother about it when she was an elderly woman.

Sancho and Moses were close. It seems they grew up together. In an affidavit for Moses's disability pension claim, Sancho said he and Moses lived on the same plantation in Bluffton before the War. In a deposition from 1898, Moses said they were raised together in the same house. It's unclear which plantation they were enslaved on. Moses said he was born in Bluffton, South Carolina, as "the slave of Dr. Kirk" but when Kirk's estate was divided, he became the slave of Theodore Coe and was separated from his father. Moses's loss of his father shows clear evidence of the ways family members were torn from one another during enslavement. Dr. Kirk was a wealthy enslaver who owned Rose Hill Plantation in Bluffton and co-owned Cherry Hill Plantation just south of Fish Haul Plantation. Moses also served together in the 21st Regiment of the US Colored Troops. The two had small farms near each other after the war.[15]

The transformation of existence that Sancho, Adam, and Jacob experienced in liberation is probably greater than any transition their descendants have made. Sancho went from enslaved legal "property" on a cotton plantation to risking his life to become an armed member of the US Colored Troops, surviving a boating accident that killed most of the men with whom he served. He played a role, along with other members of the 21st regiment of colored troops, in one of the many endings to the Civil War, celebrating emancipation on what became known as Decoration Day. Smallpox killed about 25 percent of the four million enslaved between 1862 and 1870.[16] Sancho was hospitalized in Hilton Head in 1865 from smallpox and survived it.[17]

Sancho got married, had a daughter and grandchildren, learned to read and write and was able to exercise his rights as a citizen and voter. He had the honor, like his brothers-in-law, of having his name inscribed in a wall at the African American Civil War Memorial in Washington, DC, alongside other members of his regiment.

ABOVE: My second great-grandfather's name, listed as Christopher Sancho, on the African American Civil War Memorial in Washington, DC.

RIGHT: My daughters (*left to right*) Fabiola and Maya standing in front of the African American Civil War Memorial.

His life in enslavement seems so distant, yet in some way not distant at all. My grandmother told me a few decades ago that she remembers when she and her mother were living in Savannah and her grandmother, Molly, came to live with them. Grandma was a young child—maybe four or five years old. "I've come to lay my bones with you," is what Grandma remembered Molly telling her mother Sarah when she arrived. Molly was letting her know that she was preparing to die and wanted to live with her in her last days. Grandma was five when Molly died.

And Molly always kept her hair covered. She told my grandmother that she kept it covered because people would call her an Indian and harass her if she wore it out. While that story may be possible, it seems likely that it was the kind of story that old folks tell children when they don't want to explain something that's either complicated or that children aren't thought to be ready for. Grandma didn't know that Molly lived into early adulthood as an enslaved person on Fish Haul Plantation. Molly and her daughter, my great-grandmother Sarah, must have decided to handle that past with silence and let any memories of enslavement die.

A photo taken on Fish Haul Plantation in 1862 during the Civil War by Civil War photographer Henry P. Moore showed that after the Battle of Port Royal, all the women kept their hair covered with head scarves or head wraps in West African tradition. Some of the scarves in the photo were twisted and coiled to create a more elaborate wrap. So I suspect that Molly was simply following the tradition she'd grown up with and kept her hair covered in the 1920s.

Another important detail about Molly is her complexion, which was unusually light among a family of mostly brown and dark brown people. While Molly's brothers, Adam and Jacob, were described in pension documents as dark-skinned Black men, my grandmother described Molly as "1,000 times" lighter than me with long hair that hung down her back. I am a light-skinned Black man.

Formerly enslaved men, women, and children at Fish Haul Plantation in 1862 when their status as freedpeople was still unresolved. Although my ancestors must be there it's unclear which faces are theirs. Photo by Henry P. Moore. Library of Congress, Prints and Photographs Division.

Several years ago, Cousin Eileen told me she learned from her mother Mabel (who was one of my grandmother's older sisters) that Molly's father was white, which makes the significant difference in appearance from her brothers seem logical. Molly having a white father cannot be a surprise given that most African Americans with roots in enslavement have white ancestry that came primarily through the rape of enslaved women. Molly's complexion and her hair texture appear to provide evidence.

In pension documents, Molly names her parents, Venus and Charles.[18] While it seems likely that Charles was considered Venus's husband and probably raised Molly as his daughter, he must not have been her biological father. Venus must have been haunted with tremendous emotional pain about carrying a baby conceived through such trauma. And Charles must have had intense rage about the violation of his wife's body and felt humiliation about his inability to protect her. Molly might have carried shame throughout life at the brutal act that led to her birth, which left an obvious imprint of white paternity on her body. Understandably, this wasn't something anyone in the family wanted to talk about. But Aunt Mabel one of Molly's granddaughters knew the truth and revealed it to her daughter Eileen.

All the other details of Molly's life come from written records. She wrote about her origins on a Hilton Head plantation in two letters to the US Bureau of Pensions in an effort to establish her identity so she could obtain her widow's pension and seek an increase in pension benefits after Sancho died. No birth certificate or official documents were produced when the enslaved were born, so it would have been difficult if not impossible to know her exact birth date.

In one letter dated December 12, 1916, Molly wrote:

> Dear Sir ... In 1870, I lived on Hilton Head Island, Beaufort County, State of South Carolina. This is the place where I have born. Place is Drayton Plantation. Here on Hilton Head we have no street, no number and no ward. My father's name was Charles Jenkins and my mother's name was Venus Jenkins. My brother's names are Adam Jenkins, Jacob Jenkins and my sister's name is Hager Jenkins, they are all dead. I was living with my parents.[19]

A couple of months earlier, in a separate letter to the Pensions Bureau, Molly was clearly trying to clear up confusion about her exact age.

In the letter dated October 24, 1916, Molly uses the other name for Drayton Plantation, Fish Haul, to explain her difficulty in trying to determine her age; she states that she is relying on the memories of family members to help figure it out. In that letter, she also talks about being destitute when Sancho died a couple years earlier.

Dear Sir: I received your letter stating that I have not attained
the age of 70. After the death of my husband, I was so over
burdened with debt and destitute until I never take any time to
seek about my age. Now, since finding out my age, the date that
my mother had, I am over 70 years. My mother was burned out
causing her to lose the date of my birth, but my brother has it in
one of his old book. I may be older and I may be younger. I don't
know. I only have to take what they have told me. Long time
after the fire they were talking about my age and my mother
said that she could remember the year I've born in 1840, in
the month of March. I am right to the very place I born—but
not to the very spot. The place that I born is called Fish Hall
plantation, right near the sea shore. I am not a war widow. My
husband and I was in gage [*sic*] to be marry the very year he
was ingage for the army. The first church that I have joined,
the church is destroyed and all of the old officers are dead
out. There are only two of us now living. Yours respectfully,
Margaret Christopher.[20]

In the federal census of 1870 for Hilton Head, Margaret Christopher's age is listed as 22. Her occupation is listed as "keeping house."
She was sharing a household with Simco, 24, and 5-year-old Isabella.
Simco's occupation is listed as a farmer. "Simco" was probably the
census taker's approximation of the name Sancho gave when asked.

An earlier record of Molly's life while enslaved is provided in a
document from December 1857 when the owner of Fish Haul Plantation, Mary B. Pope, died and Thomas F. Drayton, as executor of
her estate, created an inventory of her property that listed enslaved
people as part of the personal estate. Molly's family was grouped together on the inventory except for Charles, whom she identified decades later in the application for a widow's pension as her father. The
amount their lives were considered to be worth was listed next to

their names. Venus was valued at $500. Young Hagar, Molly's sister, was valued at $700. Her brother Jacob was valued at $700. Adam was $900. And Margaret (Molly) is valued at $300. One enslaved elderly woman, Old Hagar, was not considered to be worth anything by Drayton, as denoted by a dash listed next to her name in the column where the monetary value was recorded.

Mary B. Pope had willed the enslaved people on her plantation to her grandchildren, the children Thomas F. Drayton had with her daughter, Emma Catherine Pope. Included in the list of Mary Pope's property was $15 found in her purse and the proceeds from four bags of Sea Island cotton that netted $169.70, five bales of cotton that netted $625.13, and another five bales that sold for $462.79.

My Great-Great-Uncle Adam Jenkins

The details of Adam's life in enslavement are almost nonexistent. But one man he served with in the US Colored Troops who had been enslaved on Fish Haul Plantation said in a September 21, 1910, deposition that he remembered the day Adam was born. The man, Minus Chisolm (also known as Minus Drayton), said he was the one who summoned the granny—an enslaved midwife—to alert her that Adam's mother was about to deliver.[21]

An inventory of the estate of Mary B. Pope from 1857 that includes the estimated value placed on the lives of my ancestors, Venus, Margaret (Molly), Hagar, Adam and Jacob and others enslaved at Fish Haul Plantation.

On November 4, 1901, thirty-five years after Adam Jenkins was discharged from the Union Army, he discussed having been enslaved in his pension application to the US Bureau of Pensions. "I was born on Drayton Plantation; I was born a slave to Thomas Drayton who lived where I was born (he is dead)." The powerlessness of enslavement and lack of personhood before the Civil War screams through the handwritten deposition. Adam, Molly's brother, describes himself as a farmer living one-quarter of a mile from the Hilton Head post office on November 4, 1901, and relies on his former owner's son's age to figure out how old he is. "I was born right here but don't know when it was and only know my age by my old master's son's age. He was one year older than me and he is 59 years old."[22]

The fact that Adam only knew his age in relation to his enslaver's son's age shows that his life only had value to his enslaver and the larger society for the labor it produced. His humanity wasn't recognized. The ability to mark such a consequential day in one's life—the birth of one's child—was withheld from Adam and his mother Venus. She, like most enslaved, would have been kept illiterate without the ability to know or keep track of significant dates. Simply surviving every day amid such powerlessness had to have been her priority. Adam's life, like Jacob and Sancho's and his sister Molly's, didn't exist in the society of the free. It only existed among those confined in enslavement. "Social death" is the term Harvard University sociologist Orlando Patterson used to describe one's existence during enslavement. He explains that the enslaved had no recognized rights to their own lives. "Because the slave had no socially recognized existence outside of his master, he became a social nonperson," Patterson wrote.[23] Adam's existence, while enslaved, was clearly that of a nonperson, the enslaved walking dead. But somehow, he and his family affirmed their lives and value to whatever extent they could.

Adam names his mother as Benis in the deposition from 1901, which indicates her name was probably not actually Venus. "Charles

Jenkins was my father and Drayton was his master. Benis Jenkins was my mother and Drayton was her master." Adam also mentions that his father had been bought by a man whose last name was Jenkins and that's how he ended up with the last name of Jenkins.[24]

Adam indicated that his deposition was his accurate sworn statement by marking an X on the line where a signature was expected in his depositions from 1897 and 1901. Perhaps he never became literate. He enlisted on April 24, 1863, like his twin brother Jacob and Sancho in Company A of the 3rd Regiment of the US Colored Troops, which was later changed to Company E of the 21st Regiment.[25] Adam was probably 20 years old at enlistment, based on what he said in depositions decades later. At enlistment, he was thought to be about 23 years old and 5 feet, 7 inches tall, with black hair and eyes and a dark complexion.

Adam was accused of deserting the army in February 1864, six months after signing up. But he returned to duty by May and began receiving pay in June. The details of his Civil War service do not reveal a great deal about his wartime experiences. Adam was charged $9.30 for losing equipment. And, like his brother-in-law

Many US Colored Infantry volunteers enlisted at the army recruitment center in Hilton Head, located to the left of the Port Royal Restaurant. National Archives and Records Administration.

Sancho, he also survived a bout of smallpox after being treated at a smallpox hospital.

Details of Adam's life after the war reveal clear ambition and determination to improve his material condition and live with dignity. Like his twin brother Jacob and his brother-in-law Sancho, Adam got married when the war ended. On September 7, 1866, just five months after his discharge, it appears Adam became a landowner. On that day Adam Jenkins bought 5 acres of former plantation land for $15 on Port Royal Island some 32 miles from Hilton Head. And one month later on October 5, he bought 10 acres for $15, according to an index of land certificates compiled by the Heritage Library.[26] It's unclear how Adam might have used that land. The land he bought was made available through Insurrection Acts, passed by Congress during the Civil War in 1862 and after the war in 1866, which allowed plantation land in areas that had rebelled against the federal government to be seized and sold to men and women who were the "head of a family and colored citizens." Adam had plenty of company among the newly freed Black men and women owning land. Some 2,000 bought small parcels on Sea Islands in Beaufort County, mostly between 5 and 20 acres, for about $1.50 an acre, the index indicated.

Adam became a tax-paying landowner. He registered to vote and was listed in the 1868 voter's list for Hilton Head among 1,000 "colored" men. Adam was exercising political power that was unimaginable for Black people just a short time before. He had the distinction of joining the fight for his freedom and owning a home in Mitchelville, the only self-governing town established by the federal government for Black people.

In 1868, after years of toiling on a plantation as someone's property, his life once valued at $900, he was farming for himself on Hilton Head. According to the agricultural census of 1868, Adam was among a few hundred Gullah-Geechee farmers in Hilton Head growing long-staple cotton, rice, sweet potatoes, corn, peas or beans, and tobacco. Adam had 8.5 acres under cultivation and

2.5 acres planted. He had grown 25 pounds of long-staple cotton, planted a half-acre of rice and produced 5 bushels from that half acre. He'd planted 4 acres of corn, producing 30 bushels and a half-acre of peas or beans, producing 3 bushels. He had a hog and produced 100 bushels of sweet potatoes. He indicated his farm equipment was worth $200.

In 1868, when Adam's name showed up in the agricultural census, it was a time when he said he could "do good work." I don't know what his life was like after the early post–Civil War years. But in 1897, Adam discussed his health problems from epilepsy and rheumatism and how it ruined his ability to work.

"I am now receiving a pension at the rate of $12 per month on account of falling fits, (epilepsy). I was taken with those fits for the second year after I went into the army. I can give you very little information about these fits, I had no warning, no headache, no sick stomach. I would lose consciousness and fall down."[27]

Adam said he was having "fits" about every month in the army in the 1860s but could resume work after two to three days. But in 1897, when he was 56 years old, they were less frequent, occurring about every other month but he needed about one month to recover. In a deposition taken March 17, 1897, he describes pain in his side, back and shoulder that he attributes to rheumatism and having vision problems. "I consider that I am disabled one half of any time by rheumatism . . . I cannot work much of any time without stopping to rest," he stated. "And at times I have to quit and come to the house. Am unable to do much labor. Taking one year with another since the war I have been more or less disabled. When I first came out of the army, for five years, I could do good work." He said he used to fish but no longer does so because it troubles his illness.[28]

Despite his physical limitations, Adam still farmed and invested in land. He bought 79 acres of land in 1894 from Gabriel Gardner. It seems he had bought land in Port Royal and had a small 20- by 14-foot home and lot in Mitchelville.

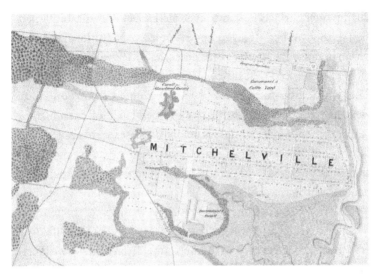

Historic map of Mitchelville, the self-governing freedpeople's town established on former Fish Haul plantation land in 1862. National Archives and Records Administration.

Both the lot and home were valued at $5, according to Thomas F. Drayton's restitution application to secure the return of plantation land to his family. Adam was one of twenty-three residents identified in tax records in 1879 in Mitchelville and ten of them, including Adam, were former US Colored Troops.[29]

After the war ended, Adam lived near where he was born on Drayton Plantation, according to his affidavits to the US Pension Bureau. Adam was married three times. The first two unions were brief; both wives died within several years of marriage. He married his third wife, Mary Smith McIntosh Pinckney, in 1886 when she was 17 or 18 years old and he was 45. They lived together until his death in 1910. Adam had biological children, but none survived. He and Mary began raising a boy, Joseph McIntosh, who had been orphaned at age two.[30]

After a pension law was amended in 1890, Civil War veterans could receive disability pensions even if the disability didn't occur during their service. Adam sought increases in his disability pension in 1897 and in 1902, but he never received additional compensation because the special examiners who reviewed his applications weren't convinced that his condition was as severe as he claimed. This wasn't uncommon. Many former colored troops on Hilton Head had to apply multiple times with several medical examinations and statements from witnesses before increases were granted.[31] In fact, Adam, like Sancho and Jacob, was fortunate to receive a pension since only about 42 percent of Black veterans who applied for benefits were successful.[32]

Adam died on February 10, 1910. If he was correct about having been born in 1843, he was 67 and didn't live a very long life. Nevertheless, the trajectory of Adam's life—from being considered property to becoming a soldier, voter, husband, father, tax-paying homeowner, landowner, farmer and resident of the only self-governing Black town created during the Civil War—is a remarkable

Gravesite of my second great uncle Adam Jenkins in Drayton Cemetery.

one. Adam Jenkins's farmland shows up on maps decades after his death in 1931 when two major investors mapped the area before buying land where both Fish Haul and Grasslawn plantations were located.[33]

Adam's gravesite is just yards from the waters of Port Royal Sound, on former plantation land where he had been enslaved, which was also land where he lived in freedom as a farmer. Adam's tombstone, with a badge engraved to signify his participation in the 21st Regiment of US Colored Troops, is just feet away from those of Sancho, who he grew up with and his twin brother, Jacob. It stands as a memorial to his service and the war that was necessary for liberation.

My Great-Great-Uncle Jacob Jenkins

Jacob volunteered to serve with his twin brother, Adam, and Sancho in the US Colored Troops on April 24, 1863; he served for three years. Jacob didn't know his age, according to his application for a disability pension, filed decades later with the US Bureau of Pensions. In a deposition on April 25, 1890, he told a pension examiner that he was about 45 or 46. "Don't know exactly," the deposition says.[34]

Like Adam, he was unable to pinpoint or celebrate his actual birthday. When Jacob enlisted he was described as a 5 foot, 6 inch, dark-skinned Black man. He said he had been the slave of Thomas Drayton.[35]

Jacob's life in slavery would change dramatically on November 7, 1861, when the Union took possession of Hilton Head within hours during the Battle of Port Royal. He, like many of the newly freed at Fish Haul, might have earned money by growing and picking cotton or maybe he sold goods to members of the military. Nearly eighteen months after the battle, he joined the US Colored Troops. But his time in the service was difficult. Although he was promoted from corporal to sergeant while serving, he also suffered a reduction in rank after being found absent without leave during a time of tension between soldiers from the 21st Regiment and Colored troops from elsewhere in 1865.[36]

During that time, Jacob was shot and seriously injured by a fellow member of the US Colored Troops after he was accused of leaving the base without permission, his pension application documents indicate. The gunshot would cause Jacob to lose his right leg. The shooting happened when Jacob attempted to reach an officers' tent to plead his case about leaving the base. Jacob believed he wasn't absent and violating military rules but had permission to leave to go to the store in Mitchelville. A provost guard shot Jacob when he disregarded the guard's order to stop as he tried to proceed to the officers' tent.[37]

Here are some details Jacob shared in 1890:

> I claim pension for the loss of [my] right leg. I was shot in the leg at Hilton Head, S.C. I cannot give the date. It was in the summertime, the summer after Lincoln was killed, the summer of 1865. It was between 7 and 8 o'clock at night that I was shot. I was going to sutler tent to get some tobacco and stuff for myself. The sutler tent was outside of camp, a short distance. . . . We had returned from Morris Island to Hilton Head expecting to be mustered out and we were allowed a good deal of liberty then by the officers. Richard Black was on guard camp ground at the time. He asked us where we was going and I told him I was going to the sutlers tent to get some tobacco and he said alright. I went to the sutler's tent. Sancho Christopher was with me at the time. . . . We stayed and we were on our way going back to camp when I was shot.[38]

Initially, Jacob had trouble receiving a disability pension. During the second examination, a pension examiner determined that the shooting was "spiteful, malicious, and wholly unjustifiable" and that

Jacob was "blameless." In addition to losing his leg, Jacob was con-fined for four months and suffered a reduction in rank. The pension documents note that the shooting and jailing happened because of conflict between soldiers of the 21st Regiment who were mostly from Hilton Head and soldiers from a different area. While the soldiers of the 21st were away fighting, another group of Colored troops sta-tioned near Mitchelville "laid siege" to the wives, girlfriends, and female family members of men of the 21st Regiment. This situation led to bad blood between the 21st and the other troops, according to Samuel Wood, a special examiner, who reviewed Jacob's pension claim.[39]

The hardship Jacob experienced while serving in the 21st Regi-ment didn't seem to blunt his ambition. In 1868, three years after the war ended, Reverend Abraham Murchison of First African Baptist Church and mayor of Mitchelville married Jacob and his first wife Catherine Pope.[40] Despite the amputated right leg, he was some-how able to manage acres of land, grow, and produce vegetables and cotton to meet his needs. The agricultural census of 1868 for Hilton Head shows that Jacob was farming on 7¼ acres of land and had used 4 acres to produce 200 pounds of long-staple cotton, ¼ acre to produce 2 bushels of rice, 2 acres of land to produce 10 bushels of corn, and 1 acre to produce 20 bushels of sweet potatoes. He had two swine and farm equipment valued at $200.[41]

Like his brother, Jacob registered to vote in 1868. He and Cath-erine moved to St. Helena and lived there for a couple of decades. In 1897, Catherine died and was buried in Hilton Head and Jacob began living in Hilton Head again. Although he was a carpenter when he enlisted and farmed, Jacob had acquired another skill at some point and began working as a shoe cobbler in 1898.[42]

At some point, Jacob learned to read and write; the signatures in his depositions are very legible but his signature gives the appear-ance that his hands were shaking when he signed, perhaps due to his limited experience with writing.

Five years later in 1902, Jacob married Mary Ann Robinson Hayward, who was about the same age and also had been enslaved on Fish Haul. In a deposition, Mary Ann said: "I married Jacob Jenkins seven days in Christmas month (Dec. 7 1902) Rev. Williams married us in the church in front of the congregation."[43]

In 1902 Jacob began receiving an $8 monthly disability pension. But on May 27, 1903, Jacob died of pneumonia. Doctors found that he had rheumatism in both shoulders, heart palpitations, dizziness, failing eyesight, and painful testicles. His pension was to be increased to $12. But there's no evidence he received it. His wife Mary Ann applied for a widow's pension but was denied because she married him after June 27, 1890, which was the cutoff date to qualify for a widow's pension.[44]

CHAPTER 7

Speaking Gullah

The only time my grandmother returned to Hilton Head (I believe it was around 1980), one of the oldest people on the island mistook her for her oldest sister, Agnes (Aggie). When she tried to explain that she was Aggie's younger sister, the elder said, "Dishere da Aggie," which translates into, "This here is Aggie." She said the person then said, "Oh you look good Aggie. You look so young."

Grandma said, "I knew what they were saying, they thought I was Aggie." But she simply smiled in response because she knew not to correct old people. That simple sentence, dishere da Aggie, would have been unintelligible to me without her translation. It showed she understood Gullah-Geechee Creole to some extent although I had never heard her speak it before then.

Having lived almost her entire adult life outside the region, I am not sure whether my grandmother could converse in Gullah-Geechee anymore. But I presume she spoke it like most who grew up in Hilton Head when the island's Black population mostly lived among themselves decades before the bridge to the mainland was built in 1956. Grandma's distance from Creole was probably typical. African Americans outside the culture so often stigmatize and ridicule people they consider Geechee and would laugh at how they spoke. Teachers who do not understand it tend to marginalize it as incorrect, improper English and misunderstand that the Gullah-Geechee Creole language, like any language, has its own rules and reasons for existing.

One way to get closer to my ancestors' world involved learning more about the language they spoke and heard all the time. Like other English-based Creoles in the Caribbean, the Gullah-Geechee Creole developed along the coast of West Africa through trade between West African ethnic groups and the English.[1] However, unlike the Creoles spoken in the Caribbean, Gullah-Geechee is not spoken as widely and openly, especially around those outside the culture because of the stigma, according to experts I spoke with. Although scholars in the 1960s recognized the Gullah-Geechee ability to retain aspects of African culture as a great achievement, helping to challenge the negative perceptions, the stigma still persists. Even people who speak Creole will characterize it as "speaking bad."

When I talked with Cousin Phoebe about the Creole, she said she always just considered it bad English. When I first visited Hilton Head as an adult in 2010, Phoebe's sister Mary spoke to me with a phrase in Gullah and she laughed when my eyes widened, and it was clear I didn't understand it. But she wouldn't repeat the phrase. And during another visit, she told me her son, Reco, could really speak that "Gullah talk." But he didn't speak it and I didn't press him to speak it.

The emergence of Gullah-Geechee, like other English-based Creoles that are common in the Caribbean, can be traced to the 1700s to a period of direct trade between the British and West Africans along the coast of West Africa. English-based Creoles, like Gullah-Geechee, mostly depend on English vocabulary but incorporate a different pronunciation for just about every word. And the structure and grammar are different from standard English and based on the African languages people on the coast spoke. Gullah-Geechee is similar in derivation to Jamaican Patois or the Creoles from the

Bahamas or Guyana. They're complete languages with consistent grammar structures, according to linguists, not broken English.[2]

Opala showed just how close the Creoles are in a folktale called *Da Fox en de Crow* recorded by writer Ambrose Gonzales in 1923.[3]

Gullah Creole:
Den, Fox staat fuh talk, E say to eself, e say,
Dish yuh crow duh ooman, enty, Ef a kin suade
Um fuh talk, him haffa op'n e mout enty?
En ef a op'n e mout, enty de meat fuh drap out

Sierra Leone Krio:
Den, Fohx stat foh tok, I sey to inself, I sey,
Dis Kro ya na umen, enti, If a kin pasaweyed
Am foh tok, I get foh opin in moht, enti
En if i opin in moht, enti di mit go fohdohm?

English version:
Then the fox started to talk. He said to himself, he said
This here crow is a woman, not so? And if I can persuade
Her to talk, she had to open her mouth, not so?
And if she opens her mouth, isn't it true the meat will drop out?

Opala also demonstrated the similarity between Gullah-Geechee and Krio by translating the phrase my grandmother spoke to me in Gullah-Geechee: Dishere da Aggie would be Dis ya na Aggie in Krio.

The connection of Gullah to Krio and the languages of Sierra Leone is particularly strong. Some 25 percent of the 4,000 African words used by the Gullah-Geechee were from languages spoken in Sierra Leone, so it's not surprising that Sancho's mother, Heena, and his father, Prince, gave him a name that may have originated there.[4] Sancho's mother's name, Heena (spelled Hina by Turner in the international phonetic alphabet that linguists use) was also listed as a name in Turner's work *Africanisms*. Hina is phonetically the same name as Heena. According to Turner, "hina" means to be obstinate in the Umbundu language of Angola and was a personal name. He found Hina to be a word in the Mende language of Sierra Leone and a word in Twi, which is spoken by the Akan peoples of Ghana.

The Lowcountry Gullah Culture Special Resource Study, which was part of the effort to establish the Gullah-Geechee Corridor, stated that some 3,595 of the 4,000 African words Turner identified were names. Turner discovered some 251 African words used in the Gullah-Geechee Creole that were not part of the naming tradition and 92 expressions in African languages showed up in prayers, songs, and stories.[5]

The Gullah-Geechee Creole allowed speakers to keep communication hidden from white people and also bonded speakers, the report's authors wrote.

> An inflection in the voice, a change in tone, could convey to a fellow black a secret thought hidden from Whites. Proverbs also conveyed subtleties and ambiguities that contributed to the survival of the people as they transmuted them into meaningful metaphors in their new environment. Songs, stories, and prayers, even with meanings obscure, kept alive dreams of a dimly remembered past.[6]

Traditionally, many Gullah-Geechee would give their children two names: an English name that was used for official purposes and with strangers and an African name known by family and friends. Sometimes the basket name was an English word but followed an African naming practice that was based on an attribute of the infant or the time of year a child was born. Charles Joyner researched naming practices among the enslaved in Waccamaw South Carolina, also in the Lowcountry, and noted the use of names reflecting the time of birth, such as Monday, Friday, March, April, Summer, or Winter.[7]

Names like Boney, Lazy, Handful, and Hardtimes reflected the child's physical attributes or characteristics or a family's situation at the time of childbirth. Gullah-Geechee people would sometimes name babies after places, like London, Paris, Dublin, or Scotland, similar to some naming practices in West Africa where children may be named after cities or villages. Titles would show up in naming practices as well, such as Doctor and Prince.[8] Prince was Sancho's father's first name, and his brother was named Paris. The authors of the National Park Service study noted that "the traditional use of basket names has important social functions within Gullah communities. For example, names form interrelationships between family and community, as well as within the larger network of kinship."[9]

My great-grandmother Sarah was called Pink, which may have been a description of her skin color at birth. And an older cousin was named Mayday but didn't like the name and changed it.

Gullah Language Today

The Gullah-Geechee Creole played a unifying role among the enslaved who derived from different ethnicities. "It helped the people to endure the harsh reality of slavery. More than any other attribute, it characterized and molded together the individuals of the sea island community forming an abiding bond of understanding among the slaves," National Park Service researchers wrote.[10]

Despite the important social value of the Gullah-Geechee creole in bonding speakers and resisting the white power structure, research has shown that the language was completely misunderstood until Turner's work *Africanisms in the Gullah Dialect* appeared in 1949 and began changing those views. Up until that time, those outside the culture and even scholars held disparaging views of Gullah-Geechee Creole, according to Katherine Wyly Mille and Michael B. Montgomery. People even considered the Creole to be evidence of inferior intellectual ability. Lowcountry white people who had heard

Gullah spoken all their lives often associated it with ignorance and cheap labor. "They had built their own theories why Gullah people were poor, or disenfranchised, or why they deserved to be these things," Mille and Montgomery wrote. Gullah speakers were first of all black, descended from Africans and African Americans branded by slavery, which had relied on a theory of their lesser humanity. . . . While their speech was sometimes described with paternalistic affection as 'colorful' and 'rhythmic,' it was popularly viewed as a failed attempt to master English."[11]

I talked with Dr. Jessica R. Berry, a speech language pathologist and Gullah-Geechee expert who speaks Creole, about her experiences growing up and the continued misunderstandings surrounding it. Berry was an assistant professor at South Carolina State University when we talked in 2018 and an advocate for preserving the language. Berry had also worked as an educational consultant, instructing schoolteachers about how to recognize Gullah-Geechee speech patterns so they could assist their Gullah-Geechee students in speaking standard English with fluency while maintaining their Creole.[12]

Berry grew up in Huger (pronounced "Hugee"), South Carolina, some twenty miles from Charleston. When discussing the features of Gullah-Geechee Creole, she easily switches between standard English and Gullah-Geechee, alternating between the relatively monotone sound of standard English to the melodious Caribbean-sounding lilt of Gullah-Geechee.

She pointed out some of the language's features. There's the universal pronoun, "e," she explained. "Instead of saying: 'He's over there or she's over there,' as you would in standard English, you might say, 'E ober dere," she said. The universal pronoun, "e," can refer to he, she, it, or them. Past tense is not generally used. In standard English, you would say: "She rode the bike fast"; in Gullah-Geechee Creole, you would say: "E ride da bike fast." The word "been," can mean was, were, and went. You might say, "I been dere all day." Words are shortened, the language is spoken rapidly, and there are distinctive Creole expressions that differ from mainstream English. Instead of telling someone to roll up the window in a car, a Gullah-Geechee speaker will say, "Up the window."

Berry's path to linguistics and speech pathology was forged by negative experiences she had in school. After growing up in a community where Gullah-Geechee was widely spoken, she encountered people in her predominantly white high school who looked down on the way she spoke. Teachers would tell her they did not understand what she was saying and that she needed to talk more slowly. Their message was clear. "I'd never be anything, speaking this way," she said. Given how she spoke, they didn't think she would be able to handle honors courses.

But Berry proved them wrong, teaching herself to code switch, alternating between mainstream English and Gullah-Geechee. No one expected teachers to recognize Gullah-Geechee speech patterns and work with her in a respectful way, she said.

When studying linguistics, she researched the origin of Gullah-Geechee Creole and how it had been traced to enslavement, the dependence on enslaved men and women from rice-growing regions of Africa, and how a form of Creole developed as a way to communicate in English. "Slaves," she said, "would teach their kids this mix of African language and English." Berry has focused research on documenting the features of the language to help school districts recognize Gullah-Geechee speech patterns. Her efforts are designed to help children translate their grammar and syntax and pronunciation to standard English.

A few years ago, South Carolina public schools were considering placing children who speak Gullah-Geechee in English for Speakers of Other Languages (ESOL) classes for second-language learners. She opposed that policy, arguing that ESOL classes for Gullah-Geechee language dominant children would feed a negative narrative that the students lacked English skills. Pejorative views among educators, she said, could impede children's education and erode the self-esteem of those who speak it as their primary language.[13]

Children who grow up speaking Gullah-Geechee, Berry explained, understand standard English because they hear it all the time, but when they don't grow up speaking it, their spoken English won't be standard English because it is not what they have practiced. Their language will reflect Gullah-Geechee speech patterns. Berry advocates that teachers understand and teach the origins of the Creole, recognize its patterns, and help children switch to standard English in a respectful manner.

"When we come in speaking Gullah-Geechee, we are automatically put into a box," she said. In response, Berry asks pointed questions: "Are you going to fix them? They speak a heritage language. Or are you going to help them learn?"

The struggle to create a level of respect for Gullah-Geechee is an internal struggle within Gullah-Geechee communities. People have grown up hearing that the Creole is bad English. You still hear Gullah-Geechee speakers saying, "I don't speak that way," said Berry. But she'll correct them and say, "Yeah, you do." "There's a pervasive negativity," she said. Her mother would tell her that people in some parts of South Carolina like the Sea Islands where the Creole seems even more pronounced were "talking bad." Her mother would tell her, "I don't talk that bad." She would disagree with her mother saying: "we all speak that way."

Campbell, who served as chairman of the Gullah-Geechee Cultural Heritage Corridor Commission and who grew up in Hilton Head, remembers that students would be punished for speaking what was considered bad English when he was growing up. "If you went to school, you learned mainstream English and would speak it perfectly by the time you graduated high school. You might go home and speak it [Gullah-Geechee Creole]. But you would speak it much less and eventually forget your Gullah." People outside of Gullah-Geechee communities would say you're "crazy, backward, or country" when they hear a person speaking Gullah, he said. "You become ashamed and start masking," Campbell explained.[14]

Murray Christopher—who I learned through my research is a cousin—grew up mostly speaking the Gullah-Geechee Creole with his family. When he entered grade school, the only thing students would hear about their language was how incorrect it was. "It was beaten out of you," Murray said, of the Gullah-Geechee Creole. "All you would hear is: 'That's incorrect. This is not how you pronounce it.'"

If you want to get closer to the original Gullah-Geechee Creole on Hilton Head Island, you have to talk to people who didn't go beyond second or third grade, whose speech patterns weren't transformed by the education system, said Campbell. A small number of people, maybe five or ten in Hilton Head, speak pure Gullah but not standard English. But the majority of people who grew up speaking Gullah-Geechee as children understand it well because they'd continue to hear their parents speak it. Others who lost it are becoming bilingual, having to relearn a language they spoke as children. "You have to learn that Gullah grammar again," said Campbell. "The vocabulary, you have to learn that too."

While people in Hilton Head, which is only 6 percent Black, may feel a strong stigma around speaking Gullah-Geechee, Campbell, who served as executive director of the Penn Center in St. Helena, says the Creole is more openly embraced there. "You go over to St. Helena and the Gullah flows, uninterrupted and there's no shame at all," said Campbell. Some 25 percent of St. Helena's 23,000 residents are Black and most, it would seem, with roots in the Gullah-Geechee community, according to the 2020 census.

"In Inner City Charleston you can talk to Black folks working in hotels and restaurants, and they'll still speak with a Gullah accent but at the same time distance themselves from the language," Campbell said. "If you ask them about Gullah, they'll say: 'Go over to St. Helena.' And it's because nobody told them who they are or taught them about their history."

Despite the stigma attached to the Creole, speaking a less prestigious language has benefits. People will choose to speak a language—even when it lacks the prestige of standard English or the Queen's English in the United Kingdom—because it expresses identity and unifies them, Mille and Montgomery wrote: "The assumption that anyone with a choice would prefer the standard variety [of English] for its social advantages is challenged by strong motivations for speaking a 'stigmatized' variety (such as Southern Drawl, Appalachian, Brooklynese) in order to demonstrate solidarity with and membership in the group that speaks it."[15]

While Gullah speakers live with an internal struggle that comes from the negative stigma, some are comfortable despite the views of outsiders. Campbell's nephew, who attended college and works as a surveyor, speaks Gullah-Geechee openly and raised his son to speak it. A teacher was thinking of recommending his nephew's son for a speech class once, said Campbell, until she met his father, and it clicked. He had a distinct way of speaking, which she realized wasn't evidence of a learning disability or speech problem.

The obvious pride in Gullah-Geechee culture I saw within my own family growing up in Queens was apparent at family get-togethers whenever my great Aunt Mabel's husband, Wilson Green, was present. To Uncle Green, Hilton Head was always home. Frequent return trips were necessary. And his English was so heavy with Gullah sounds and inflections that not only I but also his children would miss large portions of what he communicated. They'd ask Aunt Mabel to translate it for them. Uncle Green would teach his children how mainstream English phrases or commands would be said in Gullah-Geechee in Hilton Head. Cousin Eileen remembers that when he wanted to ask one of the children why they did something they should not have done, he'd say: "Wachu fa do?" In standard English, she said that would translate into: Why did you do that?

In Campbell's first book on Gullah traditions, *Gullah Cultural Legacies,* he offered common idioms and phrases in Gullah-Geechee. Here is a sample:

Dog got four feet but can't walk but one road
Translation: No matter how many things you'd like to do,
    you can only do one thing at a time.

E mout na know no Sunday
Translation: His/Her mouth never rests. He/She talks nonstop.

E ain't crack e teet
Translation: He or she did not respond to a greeting.[16]

The commonality of sound and grammar between Gullah-Geechee and Creoles spoken in the Caribbean Islands, former British colonies where descendants of enslaved Africans live, is clear to speakers of the Creoles and can generate a sense of shared culture and experience. When Berry attended college, she had a friend from the Virgin Islands, and the two both felt they spoke the same language.

"Gullah people tend to move toward the Caribbean people," Campbell said, as he discussed the cultural affinity. Campbell knows a Gullah-Geechee man who married a Caribbean woman and the two lived in Brooklyn. When he went to a Caribbean restaurant, he'd get a lot of free meals and once asked why it kept happening. The response: "You my countryman," said Campbell. "They thought he was from the Caribbean."

CHAPTER 8

Life before and after the Bridge

❖

No living person has done more to preserve Gullah-Geechee culture and heritage than Emory Campbell. For two decades, he was executive director of Penn Center, which engages in community development, educational, and social justice projects in St. Helena's Gullah-Geechee community. Campbell was instrumental in establishing the Gullah-Geechee Cultural Heritage Corridor—in North Carolina, South Carolina, Georgia, and Florida—as a National Heritage Area. Managed by the National Park Service, areas within the corridor are designated as heritage areas because of their national cultural and historic significance.

Campbell also worked with his friend, Joseph Opala, to bring Gullah-Geechee people to Sierra Leone. One project that brought both groups together resulted in a documentary, *Family Across the Sea,* which aired on PBS.[1]

I sat down with Campbell in his dining room for hours to learn about the Hilton Head of his youth. Although we didn't know each other, he knows my cousins, Phoebe and Sam. And I would later find that our family connections go back many generations. Campbell's ranch-style home lies tucked off a busy road in the Spanish Wells section of Hilton Head. When I pulled into the entrance of his family property, a sense of quiet descended as I drove along dirt-and-gravel paths amid the shade of tall trees. Within a stone's throw of his house are homes his brothers own. The land, he would explain, with no fences or demarcation to distinguish yards or individual lots, is very much a kinship-based family compound, reflecting the close family relationships of Gullah-Geechee culture and the approach to sharing land ownership and physical space. Four of Campbell's brothers built homes on land that has been in the family since the immediate aftermath of enslavement.

Emory Campbell at his home in the Spanish Wells section of Hilton Head.

"After slavery, we farmed all this area you see," he said, referring to the land surrounding their property. Campbell's family history on Hilton Head goes back to his great-great-grandfather, Phillip Friend Campbell, whom everyone called Friend. "He was a stickler for land ownership," Campbell said, "and ended up owning most of Spanish Wells." Friend owned more than 100 acres of land. He would sell land to other families and the history of those sales is still present today, he said, explaining that most tracts in Spanish Wells trace back to him.[2]

The name, Spanish Wells, is believed to have originated during colonial times when Spanish colonizers found springs or wells that provided fresh water as they traveled on ships between Florida and Virginia, according to the Heritage Library History and Ancestry Research Center. But I suspect the resonance as a name may also be linked to Spanish Wells Plantation, which is one of two dozen cotton plantations that existed on Hilton Head before the Civil War.

Campbell is tall and lean and seemed younger than his 77 years in the summer of 2018 when I first met him. His relaxed, warm, and friendly demeanor made conversation easy as he reflected on both the past and present. He told me he never thought he'd play a national role in attempting to preserve Gullah-Geechee history and culture. This mission began in the 1970s when many Gullah-Geechee in the region were suffering from roundworms and parasites that were caused by having to live in unsanitary conditions. "All of them had the same problems," he said. "Outhouses and no sewage at all. The same culture and the same history, caused by the same system."

After he graduated with a master's degree in environmental engineering from Tufts University, he was recruited to work in Beaufort and Jasper Counties to expand access to safe drinking water, functional sewer systems, affordable housing, and food. He helped obtain grants to install septic tanks and get people connected to safe water systems in both counties. Campbell connects the lack of safe drinking water and functional sewage to a system that had always disempowered and neglected the needs of Black people. Gullah-Geechee in the region, including my relatives, traditionally used outhouses. Drinking water was accessed through water pumps connected to underground wells that pulled water from the high water table below the ground's surface. But too often, Campbell found the water wasn't sanitary enough, if the wells were too shallow. After working on water and sewage issues, Campbell was recruited to work as executive director of Penn Center, which was founded as Penn School by northern missionaries in 1862 during the Civil War. It was one of the first academic schools for the newly emancipated in the South.

In 1980, when Campbell started working at the Penn Center, he began addressing educational needs through after-school programs. Gentrification was starting to lead to so much land loss that he also began working to help people hold on to their property. And that work led to his focus on the preservation of Gullah-Geechee culture and heritage. "The biggest surprise was how many people were looking for that Gullah history and culture and came there looking for it," said Campbell. He decided to switch from a focus on environmental engineering to cultural research. "I got busy studying my own culture," he said. Everything written about the Gullah culture he had experienced, including the foodways, the language, the spirituality, and the crafts. He had watched his grandmother knit nets for cast-net fishing every day. He had seen people making baskets. "I got labeled as the Gullah expert," he said. "Eventually, I got well versed in it."

In an article Campbell wrote of the benefits of a "renaissance" of interest in Gullah-Geechee culture, stemming from the passion among Black people during the civil rights movement to learn more about their African ancestry and roots. The interest among African Americans in their heritage occurred together with a greater interest among scholars who researched everything from the Creole language to the spiritual and music traditions. Turner's *Africanisms in the Gullah Dialect* was a key source for many scholars. The greater understanding of the culture and its contributions has also inspired a strong sense of pride among many Gullah-Geechee that's visible in Gullah-Geechee celebrations and heritage festivals along the coast from Wilmington, North Carolina to Jacksonville, Florida. The establishment of the Gullah-Geechee Heritage Corridor and many efforts at cultural preservation also reflect these changes.[3]

Because of increased national interest, Campbell and his brothers started a touring company, Gullah Heritage Trail Tours, in 1996 to offer an overview of Gullah-Geechee heritage and culture in Hilton Head because they knew the history was vanishing. They decided to tell the story of daily life on Hilton Head before the bridge to the mainland was built to give visitors a more nuanced sense of what Gullah-Geechee life was like.

The visitors who came to the island had two beliefs, said Campbell. They thought there were no Black people. Or they thought all the Black people were here and then sold the island to white people. When the brothers began giving tours, people were surprised to learn that more land was Black owned than they thought. But they had to explain that while the island's residents were once almost all Black, Black people never owned most of the island.

The brothers decided to tell the story of several neighborhoods to convey a sense of Gullah-Geechee life: Spanish Wells had people who transported people and goods. Charlie Simmons had a store and a couple of boats; he ran a private ferry. People in Gardner were medicine experts. A guy named Aiken who had a deep understanding of herbal medicine could heal horses. In Chaplin, people would go to the beach for church picnics. Chaplin farmers were able to harvest watermelon and beans earlier than people in other parts of the island because they were great farmers and always produced crops before the average farmer. In Baygall and Mitchelville, they had drum fish in March and April. They were huge fish. "They'd chop a piece off," he said, "and sell it from the back of a wagon."

Natural Healing

When my grandmother was growing up in the 1920s, Hilton Head didn't have any medical doctors. When her older sister, Mabel, suddenly fell ill with lockjaw, a root doctor helped her recover, Grandma recalled. People visited root doctors, like "Doctor" Willie Aiken, who Cousin Mary believed to be a relative, for help with anything from arthritis to a virus that wouldn't go away.

Doctor Willie Aiken, also called "Brankie," and his father, James, were well known for their mastery of the medicinal power of herbs. Gullah people in Hilton Head knew Willie Aiken as the "medicine man." He would boil potions, bottle them, and sell homemade remedies made from roots and herbs. His knowledge of herbal remedies and medicine was passed down from elders and his medicine worked.[4]

The herbal cures that root doctors relied on to a large extent derived from a healing tradition involving the knowledge of plants and animals that enslaved Africans brought to America and passed on to future generations. The enslaved didn't generally have access to doctors and had to heal themselves, according to Faith Mitchell, a medical anthropologist who studied herbal medicine traditions through the Sea Islands in the 1970s. "Given the isolation and size of the Sea Island plantations, it is obvious that the slaves were responsible for their own medical care," she wrote, noting that the plantations were devoid of plantation owners during the hot summer months.[5]

Natural healers depended on roots, teas, barks, berries, leaves, and herbs to heal physical ailments. And knowledge of effective treatments was transferred from enslaved Blacks and white enslavers. "Despite the apparent differences, however, plantation medicine certainly influenced black folk medicine. By the same token, black herb medicine certainly influenced White folk medicine, since blacks doctored Whites as well as other blacks," Mitchell wrote.[6]

The reliance on root doctors continued well into the twentieth century. In addition to addressing physical illnesses, spiritual illnesses and occult medicine were also practiced in the Sea Islands. Difficulty landing good employment or feeling you were consistently having bad luck or having conflict with family members could be reasons to receive spiritual healing. The treatment could involve a verbal blessing, a "laying on of hands," from someone with the ability to connect with God's healing powers. A conjurer could use their "powers" and words and objects to produce an illness by putting a hex on someone. Amulets would be used to protect those wearing it. The hex might cause the affected person to act in a noticeably odd or quirky manner or have stomach pain or headaches. Or the victim might feel a strong compulsion to leave town.[7]

I didn't talk with anyone who was aware of conjurers who cast spells in Hilton Head. But Dr. Jessica Berry, the Gullah-Geechee language expert, said the practices are very much alive in her hometown, Huger. Spells and magic are used for healing, for love, or for vengeance against an enemy. "It's unspoken," Berry said. "But you know who to go to."

In nearby St. Helena, one root worker or conjuror, Dr. Buzzard, had customers around the nation who sought his medicinal cures. It's believed he could command spirits and witches, attract love, heal mental illness, and protect people from evil spirits. People feared Dr. Buzzard. It was believed that his roots could take lives: If he used a mixture of roots and herbs to cast a spell on a man, the man's life could be over.[8]

+ + +

The Squire Pope community was known for its shrimpers and boatmen, said Campbell in our 2018 interview discussing the experiences of Hilton Head's watermen. Some of them would leave by boat in October, when the weather got cold and fishing was more difficult, and head to warmer waters in Florida—perhaps Key West, Amelia Island near Jacksonville, or even Corpus Christi, Texas. They would live in Florida or Texas for a few months, selling fish, and then return to Hilton Head in the summer. Some had their own boats. Others would captain a boat for someone else in the beach communities where they lived. The work could be dangerous. One of the shrimpers, who died several years ago, would tell dramatic stories about taking his boat to the Yucatan in Mexico and struggling to navigate the waters. "He almost lost his boat," said Campbell. "They didn't know how treacherous the water was."

Campbell was in high school in 1956 when the bridge to the mainland was built. Back then it was all about subsistence living, he said. Everybody took care of themselves as needed. "We grew sweet potatoes, watermelon, beans, peas, okra, sugar cane, benne [a variation of sesame seeds], and corn," he said. "And what you didn't eat, you'd sell."

People traveled by water with row boats and sailboats, he said, adding that some boats were like freight carriers. "You had men that could row a 20-foot or 30-foot rowboat," he said, "which took tremendous strength." It was a time when people would buy their produce from local growers at markets like the one on River Street in Savannah. Selling vegetables, fish, and meat for cash enabled families to buy whatever they needed that wasn't sold on the island. They would buy clothes, oil for lamps, or lumber to build a house.

In the pre-bridge days, everyone had chores to do from sunrise to sunset. Husbands were responsible for gathering food, earning money for the family, heating gallons of water on the stove and supplying it with wood, plowing farmland with a horse or mule, repairing fences, doing other household repairs, and going to their jobs every day. "The wife was just as busy. She had breakfast on the table at five or six a.m., lunch at noon, and supper at dinner time. She had housekeeping chores, cloth-making and sewing, teaching kids to cook on the wood stove, healing wounds, nurturing the garden, and, if employed, going to her normal day-to-day job."[9] And children were feeding farm animals, milking the cows, bringing them in at night, cleaning the yard, weeding the garden, and gathering pecans for sale at market.

In my interview, Campbell discussed the bartering, sharing, and communal nature of life on Hilton Head. Families had a network of people with knowledge and skills they could depend on for things they needed, he said. "We had no money, so we interdependently relied on one another to get things done." His father was a notary public. And when Campbell was growing up, some people were semi-literate or illiterate. His father might read a letter they received and help them write a response, if necessary. And if they didn't have the nominal fee he might charge, he'd tell them: "Well, bring me some fish or some potatoes." No food was wasted in the Campbell family. Twelve children needed feeding. His mother taught school to bring in some extra cash. Campbell's father was one of the many men from Hilton Head who helped dredge the Savannah River for the Army Corps of Engineers. Some men worked for the oyster businesses run by the Toomers and Hudsons, two of a handful of white families on Hilton Head. It's important to understand Black people before the civil rights movement were the laborers in the South, both skilled and unskilled, said Campbell. "Anything you wanted done— Black people were doing it."

Another Gullah-Geechee community, one that had the most commerce, was called Stoney. "It was the part of the island you would come to first, where the first traffic light was installed. The whole area was lined with stores and shops. The post office was in that area. It was where you would buy all the stuff you didn't grow— soda, ice cream, cookies, what we called 'city food'," said Campbell.

Earning and saving money was necessary for upward mobility. Families used cash to send their children to St. Helena or Beaufort to attend high school because Hilton Head didn't have a high school in the early 1950s before the bridge was built. "Life was tough," said Campbell. "That's why no one wanted to live here." Leaving was the goal for many. "People had to leave to attend high school or college. They might join the military and only come back once in a while to visit family members."

Black people on Hilton Head were locked out of an economic and political system that was controlled by white people, limiting opportunities for significant development, Campbell explained. And while the daily humiliations of Jim Crow, like segregated water fountains, bus stations, pools and parks, and restaurants weren't present, a racialized, white-dominated power structure was still operating in the background, like ghosts, haunting lives in ways you couldn't see but could feel. The marginalization of the people of Hilton Head who had been there since their ancestors were considered property would become extremely apparent in the 1950s, when plans to buy most of the island and develop vacation resort and retirement communities were being drawn up without their knowledge or involvement.

Witnessing the Bridge to Gentrification

The seeds of gentrification and the radical transformation of the island were sown decades before the 1950s, when wealthy northern businessmen learned of rich forested land with bountiful game in the Georgia Sea Islands. These men began buying large tracts of land along coastal islands of South Carolina that would be used by private hunting clubs.[10]

The first change in Hilton Head began around the turn of the twentieth century, when a Beaufort County hunting club bought 1,000 acres of land in Hilton Head that was once Leamington Plantation. The game there was plentiful. A New England investor,

W. P. Clyde, acquired 9,000 acres, buying up whatever land he could for one or two dollars an acre from the island's Gullah-Geechee residents. Land was dirt cheap. The dollar value of the land had not changed since the Civil War. So in real terms, accounting for inflation, the land had decreased in value, if you consider that people were buying land for a couple dollars an acre after the Civil War. The land's market value, after all, was determined by what subsistence farmers among the Gullah-Geechee could pay. Clyde sold the land to a wealthy New York investor, Roy Rainey, in the 1920s. Rainey ended up with half the island but had to sell the land after losing substantial wealth during the stock market crash. In 1931, Alfred Loomis, a Wall Street businessman, and his brother-in-law and business partner, Landon Thorne, bought Rainey's land at $6 an acre and eventually ended up with two-thirds of the island. Thorne and Loomis added to what they'd acquired from Rainey, buying small plots of land from island residents.[11]

When the men decided to have maps drawn of the island to identify landowners, my ancestors' names show up repeatedly, demarcating their farmland. Among the names are my great-grandmother Sarah Polite, her mother Maggie Christopher (who must be my second-great-grandmother), Margaret "Molly" Christopher, and Molly's brother Adam Jenkins.

In the early 1930s, Gullah-Geechee life was largely unchanged from what it had been in the aftermath of the Civil War. Black folks still lived primarily in the northern part of the island, fishing and farming, as they had since the Civil War. "The few wealthy northerners that owned land would come down to hunt and leave," Campbell explained. "They came and played and left." Island residents could hunt on Loomis's and Thorne's land without a problem. In the 1930s and 1940s, Hilton Head still lacked electricity, indoor plumbing, paved roads, and telephones. "They didn't do anything to develop the island in the early part of the twentieth century," said Campbell. "They never did anything for us."

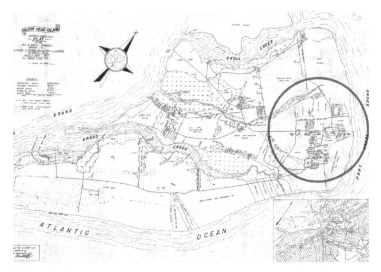

A map from 1931 prepared for two businessmen, Alfred Loomis and Landon Thorne, who sought to buy land from Hilton Head's Gullah-Geechee residents. Included in the circled cluster of landowners in Mitchelville are the names of my great-grandmother Sarah Polite, my second great uncle Adam Jenkins and my second-great-grandmother Maggie Christopher. Map courtesy of Hilton Head's Heritage Library History and Ancestry Research Center.

In the 1940s, greater awareness of the significant number of pine trees in Hilton Head spread among those who didn't live there. And harvesting those trees on huge portions of Hilton Head would lead to the eventual development of that land as gated retirement and resort communities.[12] Joseph Fraser, who owned Fraser Lumber Company, and Fred Hack, who identified properties for lumber companies, initially visited Hilton Head in 1949 hoping to lease 8,000 acres of land on the southern third of the island to harvest trees. (In 1949, the island's Gullah-Geechee residents owned about 3,200 acres of land.[13]) But the owners of the land, Loomis and Thorne, wanted to sell. Fraser and Hack then formed the Hilton Head Company and bought the 8,000 acres for $60 an acre and harvested the timber. In 1951, Hack and another man, Olin T. McIntosh, a businessman and associate of Fraser, bought Loomis and Thorne's remaining 12,000 acres in 1951 and formed Honey Horn Plantation. Although the two began building wealth by cutting down pine trees and selling millions of feet of lumber, Hack later said that while the two were selling timber on Hilton Head, he was envisioning a future "real estate bonanza."[14]

During this period in 1950, only 1,100 Black people and 25 white people lived on the island, less than the number who lived there in the late nineteenth century.[15]

The lack of economic viability for Black subsistence farmers on this undeveloped island came face to face with a completely different reality, white entrepreneurs who could wield political influence, secure massive loans, and turn Hilton Head into an island of dreams for wealthy, overwhelmingly white people who could seal themselves off from the island's Black Gullah-Geechee people and heritage.

In 1951, the Hilton Head Company was able to get the first electric lines erected. By 1953, a state representative from Beaufort County helped Fraser and Hack work with the help of the South Carolina Highway Department to establish a state-run ferry service. But the ferry could transport only nine cars at a time. To attract buyers, they would need to make it easier for cars to come to the island.[16]

State Representative J. Wilton Graves, who represented Beaufort County, began working on a plan to build a mile-long bridge to the mainland. Graves couldn't convince state officials that the project should be a priority. But he got a bill passed in 1954, authorizing the Hilton Head Toll Bridge Authority to perform bridge maintenance if a bridge were built. Hack and another developer successfully pushed a plan to finance bridge construction with private funds.[17]

The bridge opened in May 1956 and within a year 200,000 people had visited the island. Just five years earlier, Hilton Head's population was less than half the 2,500 who lived there in 1880. The independent fishing and farming lifestyle that had dominated island life was dwindling. It would further decline over the next decade and be replaced by menial jobs in the resorts, gated communities, and hotels. The Hilton Head Company sold its first beachfront lots in 1956 with prices starting at $1,100.[18] Joseph Fraser's son, Charles, would become the mastermind of the new Hilton Head, executing a vision for a massive upscale leisure and retirement community. In 1957, a year after the bridge was built, the Sea Pines Plantation Company was incorporated, with a plan for residential communities, a yacht club, beach club, golf course, recreational facilities, and a forest preserve built on seven square miles of the island.[19] Charles Fraser hired a Harvard professor and landscape architect who translated his vision for Sea Pines where the natural environment, beaches, parks, and wildlife preserves would dominate the manmade environment. Mosquitoes were so intense that he hired a state entomologist to develop a mosquito control program.[20]

A chronology of the island's transition to a resort community illustrates how Hilton Head would change dramatically over the course of a couple of decades. The first oceanfront lots at Sea Pines sold for $5,350 in 1957.[21] Fraser sought to attract upper-income clients and then transition vacationers to year-round residents.

Sea Pines would bring in the wealthy, including corporate leaders and high-ranking military officers. Sea Pines opened the first modern hotel, the William Hilton Inn, in 1959, hoping to lure visitors into buying lots. A year later, Sea Pines opened the first golf course. Fraser created the Sea Pines Public Service District in 1964 to provide sewer, water and fire protection for residents. It already had private security guards operating as a police department within Sea Pines.[22] But attracting more people, especially retirees to live at Sea Pines year-round necessitated having a medical facility on the island. Trips to Savannah or Charleston were required for medical exams with specialists. Fraser built the first clinic to solve that concern in 1965. Another issue for Fraser involved education. The children of Hilton Head's new white residents were traveling by bus to either a public school in Bluffton or a private school in Savannah.

So Fraser helped open Sea Pines Academy in 1966.[23] By 1969, ocean-front lots were selling for $50,000.[24]

The services that catered to the upper class and wealthy lay ensconced behind gates, with access restricted to residents and employees. This lifestyle of gated luxury and almost exclusively white residents was replicated throughout much of Hilton Head—from the 4,000-acre Hilton Head Plantation and Palmetto Dunes Plantation—drawing a stark contrast with Gullah-Geechee communities that were low-income, working class, or middle class but far outside the power structure.[25]

Today, Sea Pines's website boasts some 5,000 acres and a five-mile stretch of beach, which is nearly half the length of the island. It has a 605-acre forest preserve and areas for pony and horseback rides. Visitors can go on bike tours and kayak trips; charter a sailboat or power boat; or go parasailing. There are 100 slips for sailboats and yachts. Oceanfront homes at Sea Pines were selling for as much as $17.9 million in April 2024, according to the real estate website *Redfin*.

Gullah-Geechee neighborhoods like Stoney have been swallowed up by the town with the supposed intent of reducing traffic congestion and protecting green space. In the process, town officials have bought some land below market value and are disconnecting and erasing the history of a community whose formerly enslaved ancestors bought the land after the Civil War.[26]

Few Black people are found within these gated communities. The census tract within Hilton Head Plantation indicates that 99 percent of its 10,000 residents are white, Kokal reported. The census tracts covering Sea Pines and Palmetto Dunes Plantation show its residents are 97 to 98 percent white.[27]

In Campbell's view, a form of segregation was achieved through upscale development on Hilton Head that hadn't existed in any very visible way since the Civil War. Before the 1950s, no one was excluded by a locked gate and no beach access was restricted by owners.

The people, whose enslaved ancestors were buried on Hilton Head, who lived out their lives coaxing the peas, green beans, squash, okra, and watermelon from the soil and pulling shrimp, oysters, and bass from the island's creeks and bays to feed their children, were on the periphery. It is as if the Gullah-Geechee were the outsiders looking in, Campbell said, while the land they had always known underwent tremendous changes.

He vividly remembers how clueless everyone was about the plans for Hilton Head right before the building began in the 1950s and how the Gullah-Geechee residents unwittingly aided in the gentrification and their own displacement. "These were dark ages for Black people," he said, reflecting back. "Emmett Till had just gotten killed. We were just beginning to think about civil rights. All I knew was Black people were oppressed. We were always conscious that the white people were the law and running the government."

There was virtually no news coverage relevant to life on Hilton Head, he said, just "little bits and pieces of news" in the *Beaufort Gazette* and staticky broadcasts from a radio station in Savannah. No elected representatives informed them about any planned changes. Decision making around the bridge or any aspect of the development didn't include or engage the Gullah-Geechee community. They'd hear when plans were finalized. "We got word that a bridge was going to be built," Campbell said.

White folks with plans for development seemed intimidated by Gullah-Geechee people, said Campbell. "The White people who bought the island would ride around in cars with two-way radios so they could communicate with one another. They didn't trust riding around without them." But whatever trepidation they felt didn't prevent them from seeking out information about the land from Hilton Head's Black residents who were similarly wary. Fraser and Hack and their associates would talk to native islanders to figure out who to approach about land purchases. "They would seek out people who had been here for a long time, finding out about the history of the island and who owned the land," Campbell said. Who owns that land? The reply might be: "Reggie-n-them. It's woodland. No one ever farmed it."

It wouldn't take long for the actions of wealthy white developers to spark resentment as they sought to regulate island life. The first thing that Campbell remembers enraging people was a zoning proposal from State Representative J. Wilton Graves in 1955 that would have required the small wooden homes people built to be set 100 feet back from major roads—more hidden from view. "They were talking about how the shacks couldn't be in the front," said Campbell. "They were going to have to be further back." The zoning law was proposed because the developers feared that when upper-class white people saw Black people living in shacks along the highway, they wouldn't want to buy the land. Campbell's father's white friends, who were among the few white families living on the island before the bridge, informed him of the proposal. It upset them as well. Telling people how to live and build on property that their enslaved ancestors had once worked and they now owned made them livid, Campbell explained. "The one thing that these folks were fierce about was the land and telling them what to do about the land because the land came out of slavery and land meant freedom."

Campbell remembers everyone turning out for a meeting. The people who were native islanders, including the few white people who had been there before the bridge, gave Graves "hell" for introducing the bill, he said. Graves depended on Black votes, and he knew he had to reverse course and push to repeal the offensive zoning law. There was no town government to play a role in land use issues. And the county's elected officials didn't have the authority to do much besides handle road repairs. So the developers looked to Graves, the state representative for Hilton Head, to advance their interests.

Another issue that stoked anxiety and resentment among the Gullah-Geechee involved a fence law that predominantly white county supervisors passed in majority-Black Beaufort County. The law required farmers to keep their farm animals fenced in on their own property. Hilton Head's farmers traditionally allowed cattle to roam and forage for food in the winter when less grass was available. And they would round them up in the spring to keep them on their property. Letting cattle roam in the winter enabled them to find more vegetation to eat, said Campbell. But the newcomers with visions of development made it illegal to let cattle roam, so they could protect property they were planning to develop. Although all fifty states have fence laws, which typically require farm animals to be confined in an enclosure, a few states have an "open range" doctrine that allows cattle to roam off their owners' property onto other private property, according to the National Agricultural Law Center. The burden in those states falls on people who don't want cattle on their land to enclose their property to prevent them from grazing on it.

The fence law was yet another manifestation of the many changes that would alter island life alongside the demographic changes that would make the Gullah-Geechee a small minority. Stretches of island that they didn't own but had access to, like the hunting preserves, were becoming retirement and resort communities with golf courses and private beaches. In some cases, the graveyards on former plantation land that held their ancestors' remains were sealed off in these communities, requiring Hilton Head's Gullah-Geechee to receive permission to visit gravesites.

Land loss, displacement, and gentrification along with a civic and political life dominated by mostly white outsiders would envelop Hilton Head's Gullah-Geechee culture, transforming their lives and marginalizing them on an island where their families had lived as far back as memory could travel.

CHAPTER 9

A Gullah-Geechee Family's Ties

⟨⟩

While my initial knowledge of the family's heritage in Hilton Head came through my grandmother and her eldest sister, Aunt Aggie, an unbroken connection to the island's culture and heritage dating back some 200 years came through one of Aggie's five siblings—Aunt Julia.

Cousin Phoebe

Arthur Eugene Wiley and Aunt Julia had more children than all Julia's other five siblings put together. Very large families of 10, 11, and 12 children were common among Hilton Head's families. And Aunt Julia had 12 children who survived childhood: Phoebe, Romena, Samuel, Eugene, Mary, Margaret, Lilly, Victoria, Martha, Moses, James, and Cyrus.

Some of Aunt Julia's children—the remaining children now advanced in age—were the relatives who maintained land, ran businesses, and continued to be actively involved in the family's church while contributing to the Gullah-Geechee community. In 2010, on my first trip to Hilton Head, I sought out cousin Phoebe, who I had met as a child on my first visit there in 1969 or 1970. Phoebe is well known among the families who have been there before the changes. She began teaching in the 1950s in a two-room schoolhouse when dirt roads crisscrossed the island, several years before Hilton Head's rapid development began. After thirty years of teaching, Phoebe ran a small business, a combination gas station and liquor store along with her husband, Henry. (Henry became Hilton Head's first Black councilman after the town of Hilton Head was incorporated in 1983. He died at age 96 in 2024.)

Phoebe and her husband bought and sold land, including beachfront property. She is a dedicated member of St. James Baptist Church, which my family has attended since the 1880s, a couple decades after many made the transition to freedom.

When I met Phoebe, she hugged me like a long-lost friend or family member and told me she loved me when I left. Despite the fact that I lived my entire life hundreds of miles from Hilton Head and had only seen her as a 4-year-old on the one trip my family took to the island when we lived in Atlanta, she knew better than I how connected our lives were even though we barely knew each other. Her memories of my mother and grandmother dated back to her childhood, some seventy years earlier, when she lived in the same household with my grandmother, Ruth; my great Aunt Mabel; my great-grandmother, Sarah; and my mother, Shirley, who was an infant. They were her aunts, cousin and grandmother. Phoebe and her sister, Romena, lived in the multigenerational household in Savannah for part of the school year, so they could attend a better school than the elementary school on Hilton Head.

"I still remember the address," Phoebe recounted.[1] "1147-½ East Gwinnett Road in Savannah." That was a time right before my grandmother, Aunt Mabel, and Sarah joined the Great Migration north. That neighborhood in Savannah was an old Black community, a couple of miles from downtown Savannah, with a mix of single-family homes and attached clapboard townhouses. James, my biological grandfather (who was called Jack) would bring Phoebe to school. "I remember Jack," she said. "He would put me on his shoulders and take me to school in the morning."

Despite time, distance, and differences barely discussed among relatives who went north and those living in the South, Phoebe showed me the resilience of family bonds. She connected the dots in our family migration story with her knowledge and lived experience in a way that no other living relative could. Phoebe's early life began decades before the bridge; before electric lines and telephones; before cars and paved roads, running water, and sewer pipes. The Gullah-Geechee life that shaped her early years in the 1930s and 1940s was the life created by our formerly enslaved ancestors, the generation of Sancho, Adam, and Jacob, the lifestyle of farming, fishing, and hunting where you'd take a bateau (the Gullah-Geechee term for rowboat) to Savannah so you could sell the beans, sweet potatoes, and watermelon you grew. The first half of the twentieth century in Hilton Head was a time of root doctors and midwives, not modern-day medical facilities. It was a time of horses and buggies, not cars, a time when you had to respect your elders. A time without the presence of police and Jim Crow. Church deacons offered justice for civil offenses in the community through a system called "just law."

Phoebe explained that back then, children couldn't just give their right hand in fellowship to become full members of the Baptist church. Under the Baptist tradition, the right of fellowship is extended to those who have accepted a life in Jesus and gone through the process to become church members. When she was growing up, you had to show you had established your relationship with God over a period of many days, fasting and going out to the praying ground at night through the Gullah-Geechee tradition known as seeking.

Phoebe's life has spanned both eras, from the earlier period where the Gullah-Geechee dominated island life to the modern gentrified Hilton Head with its planned private communities. Strip malls, ranging from ordinary to upscale, dot the landscape along

William Hilton Parkway, the main drag. But still, Gullah-Geechee graveyards with headstones low to the ground crop up in places, calling attention to its hidden history. Gone are Gullah-Geechee establishments like the popular Abe's Restaurant, owned by Abraham and Charlie Mae Grant that served Gullah-Geechee dishes. The bricks in its chimney still showed the fingerprints of the enslaved who made them and handled them before the bricks hardened.

On trips that I took by myself or with my cousin Eileen from DC, I avoided venturing into the gated communities and paying for the day pass that would grant me access. I detested the concept of the privileged, excluding others, and ignoring and erasing the history of the Gullah-Geechee, my family and ancestors. I had viewed it from a distance, staying outside the locked gates. But on a few trips with my wife and children, I ventured in. During one of those visits, my wife found a restaurant through an online search where we could have a drink overlooking the water and our kids could eat. She had been telling me she just wanted a place where she could have a drink and see the water. When we first pulled up to one of these communities, a woman working at the entrance gate asked if we were a resident or in a vacation rental. I explained that we weren't staying there but only wanted to stop for a drink at the beachside restaurant. And, out of sympathy, it seemed, she reluctantly broke the rules to give us an entrance pass. "Here, hang this pass from your rearview mirror and don't tell anybody I gave it to you," she said. "I'm about to get off anyway. You can park in the restaurant lot and go as long as that pass is there."

I thanked her and we drove on, winding our way through the grounds. After we found the restaurant, parked, and got out, we immediately got the sense that we did not belong there. I remember three white men in shorts and t-shirts, staring, necks craned in our direction as if our presence didn't make sense. One of them donned a cap and sunglasses with a patch of white sunscreen on his nose. In the restaurant, we ordered drinks and an appetizer as a band of young barefooted white guys played blues. It was surreal that we were in what had been an almost all-Black island, but in an all-white space, except for us, as this white band played Black music. Before we were done with our drinks, my wife told me she was ready to go. She saw people staring and was tired of the unwelcoming eyes.

On the two other times behind these gates, one for a pony ride and another for a boat ride from Harbour Town in Sea Pines, Black people seemed invisible. My wife understandably wanted to give our daughters some child-centered fun, but we were both ill at ease on all these visits. I couldn't get past the fact that the people who looked like me and my relatives, the descendants of the enslaved, who built so much wealth for the nation, were practically excluded from these spaces. The brief visit to Sea Pines, which has a small Gullah-Geechee cemetery that dates back to enslavement, left me with a feeling of sadness and dread. It was as if my ancestors didn't want me anywhere near Sea Pines. And that heavy feeling stuck with me for a while even after I left.

Despite the radical transformation of life in Hilton Head, Cousin Phoebe has persevered. She had a successful career as an educator and as an entrepreneur along with her husband, and she maintained a commitment to church while supporting family. Phoebe is Sancho's and Molly's great-granddaughter. Tall and dignified, yet humble and warm. Laughter and smiles come easily to Phoebe. Over multiple conversations she talked about her childhood growing up on farmland passed down on her father's side of the family, the Wileys, who like our side of the family, were on Hilton Head before the Civil War. "We grew watermelon, corn, lima beans, sweet potatoes, and squash," Phoebe said, reflecting back. "We had cows, horses, and pigs and a wagon." Her parents earned income mainly from the sales of lima beans and watermelon, which you had to take to market in Savannah to sell. "There was a market near the foot of the Savannah River. There was no bridge to get you to Savannah. People had to take a boat to get there."

When Phoebe was growing up, the island's Gullah-Geechee residents used oil-burning lamps for light. When you needed water, you didn't go to the kitchen sink, you'd go outside to a water pump to draw water from an underground well. Needless to say, families didn't have a lot of money. But it seemed everybody survived and everyone had a plan, Phoebe said. She thinks of the people she grew up with in Hilton Head as smart and industrious, despite their lack of wealth and privilege. People generally had some type of special skill, some way to make money aside from selling what they grew. "Everybody could do something," said Phoebe. "You had to know how to build a house and how to build a boat. My daddy could."

All communities in Hilton Head had skilled bateau makers who would build flat-bottom row boats that ranged in length from 12 to 20 feet and were between 18 to 24 inches high. And a bateaux for transporting goods could be 24 feet.[2] In *Gullah Days,* the authors describe boatmaking and navigating the twisting waterways as the job of the enslaved before the Civil War. The enslaved would be tasked with taking plantation owners to the mainland and other islands for recreation and taking produce to market in Savannah on sailboats. During the Civil War, the Union Army depended on the formerly enslaved men's knowledge to direct travel through the waters to spy on Confederate troops and assist commercial boats.[3]

Back then, people not only took care of themselves but also helped their neighbors. When Phoebe's father caught bass, trout, or whiting, he would share the fish with his neighbors. Sharing food with neighbors was a common practice and actually necessary back then, because refrigerators didn't exist. Although food could be kept cold in underground pits, generally, what food you couldn't eat or sell, you gave away. "I know I ate good food," Phoebe said. "We ate straight from the river and the farm." They would go fishing all the time. Until a recent fall, Phoebe had been in the hospital only when she was giving birth. She attributes her good health in part to the healthy diet they had growing up, free of processed food and much sugar. "People were properly fed," she recalled. Phoebe didn't think she was fortunate in any way when she was growing up there. But now, she says she was blessed in ways she didn't understand then.

After a short time in Savannah, relatives migrated North, my grandmother, grandfather with my infant mother to Washington, DC, and Aunt Mabel and my great-grandmother to Harlem, New York. Phoebe returned to Hilton Head to the farm in the Grasslawn section, which native islanders call Grassland. It was like several areas in Hilton Head that still bear the name of the old cotton plantations located there before the Civil War. No one talked about enslavement when Phoebe was growing up in the 1930s and 1940s. Nor did they discuss how her father's side of the family, the Wileys, came to own land there.

Phoebe attended the Cherry Hill School, a one-room elementary schoolhouse in Mitchelville that is now listed on the National Register of Historic Places. It was the only elementary school on Hilton Head in a building that was intended as a school. Her father spearheaded the fundraising effort to buy the land where the county built the school in 1937. Several years later, Phoebe ended up attending a boarding school, called the Mather School in nearby Beaufort, South Carolina, where she studied from seventh through twelfth grade. Mather has its roots in the post–Civil War era, when it was founded to educate formerly enslaved girls.[4]

When Phoebe attended school in the 1940s, Hilton Head still didn't have a high school. In Beaufort, Phoebe had one of the few experiences she would ever have with Jim Crow segregation. When she'd go to the movies with her (African American) classmates, accompanied by mostly white teachers, the students could fill seats in the white section of a segregated theater there. Somehow teachers at Mather found a way for their students to avoid the humiliation of Jim Crow while attending movies. They shielded the children, she said, never discussing what segregation was all about. Phoebe said she wondered why all other Black folks besides her schoolmates were sitting upstairs in the area reserved for colored people.

She did, however, have one very memorable experience with segregation at Mather. On a field trip they took a Greyhound bus from Beaufort and teachers gave them a stern warning to stand for the entire trip and never sit down. "Maybe the other girls knew it was segregation," she said. "But I didn't." She realized years later that Black children couldn't sit down on the bus because the seats were reserved only for white people. In the virtually all-Black Hilton Head of her youth, Jim Crow segregation—unlike elsewhere in most of the South—was invisible.

Mather laid the basis for Phoebe's career as a first-grade teacher. She wanted to be a nurse but her parents, Arthur and Julia, couldn't afford to send her to nursing school or college at the time. But when she returned to Hilton Head with a high school diploma, her god-mother encouraged her to apply for a job teaching first grade in a two-room schoolhouse. Phoebe applied, got the job, and started teaching. She later worked her way through college at Savannah State University to earn her bachelor's degree in education.

At 95, Phoebe is well known among Hilton Head's Gullah-Geechee community because she taught so many children during her thirty-year teaching career. Phoebe and her husband Henry eventually sold the gas station and liquor store because none of their children wanted to take over the businesses. Like others in the Gullah-Geechee community on Hilton Head, Phoebe made it clear that she didn't think of herself as Gullah or Geechee growing up. But she spoke the Creole as a child when playing and interacting with other children.

When my parents and I visited when I was a child, we spent time in the Golden Rose Park restaurant that her brother Eugene ("Gene") owned. It was on land that was once farmland where she, Gene, and their other siblings were raised. Phoebe remembered me climbing around the restaurant and peering through a window because I was too small to easily see inside.

What I remember from the childhood trip appear in my mind like Polaroid snapshots of me standing near a pool table in the restaurant and also standing in a thicket of what seemed like a forest on what Gene told my father was my great-grandmother's land. Although my memories from the trip are minimal, my father talked about the trip many times: how impressed he was with the island's natural beauty and amazed that the island's residents were almost exclusively Black and owned so much land there. For years, a piece of twisted and gnarled dark brown wood taken from family property was in our living room, providing a silent testament to our heritage.

Dad talked of Phoebe's warmth and Gene's friendliness. My parents had checked into a hotel on that trip since my mother—who grew up in New York City—didn't know family members well and didn't want to impose. But when Gene learned that my parents were on the island, he came by the hotel, told them they were family and they would have to check out and stay with him, not in some private hotel. Gene showed them land the family once owned and what he called Mama's land that the family still owned. In referring to Mama, Gene was referring to his maternal grandmother Sarah, who was also my mother's maternal grandmother. Gene told my parents that because it was Mama's land (she had died several years earlier), they should build a house there. It hadn't been willed to anyone in Gullah-Geechee tradition and building a house was my mother's birthright.

At the time of the visit the bridge to the mainland had been built for slightly more than a dozen years, and the island's population was already majority white, privatized and off limits to Black residents who had been there. So much of the island's shore had been gobbled up by developers that Phoebe and her husband sold land to the city for a small sum, so the land could be maintained as a public park and beach. "We had beach property we practically gave to the town," Phoebe said. If she had not offered to sell the land, she said she was afraid that Black people wouldn't have a beach to go to. The land was adjacent to other beachfront property that she and her husband sold to the Marriott International, which in 2024 became the Hilton Beachfront Resort & Spa. The 11-acre Driessen Park Beach has a playground, bathroom and showers, picnic tables, and a walkway to the beach. But the town didn't follow through on all it had agreed to, like free parking. Instead, it installed meters. Still, Phoebe is glad the beach exists because public access points for local families in Hilton Head are so limited.

Daughters Fabiola (*left*) and Maya (*right*) with author at the playground at Driessen Beach Park in 2018.

Phoebe had three adult children; one son is now deceased. She has six grandchildren and three great-grandchildren. And she maintains a close relationship with her immediate family. She talks to a sister who lives in Savannah regularly. When I visited a few years ago, her brother Sam would stop by regularly and visit for a bit. A son lives down the street. A daughter who used to live nearby moved in with her. And her great-granddaughter Brea, who's fond of Phoebe, would spend a lot of time visiting with her. During the visits in Phoebe's spacious home on a half-acre lot, Phoebe talked about differences between the island she grew up on and contemporary life in Hilton Head.

Every time I've visited Phoebe or called, she tells me she loves me. I tell her I love her too. When I visited with my wife, Elena, she told her she loved her, and she was always welcome because she was also family. Phoebe's interactions show that family ties can endure, despite differences in generations, geography, and the economic needs that split my family into Northerners and Southerners.

(*Left to right*) Cousins Phoebe, Eileen, and Sam at Phoebe's house in 2010 on my first trip to Hilton Head as an adult.

Cousin Mary

Cousin Mary, who was six years younger than Phoebe, was living on more than an acre of family land that sits next to a large expanse of tidal marsh.[5] From the backyard, I could look across the wetland to the waters of Port Royal Sound where naval ships converged in 1861, ending enslavement in our family and the families of all Black Hilton Head residents whose ancestry dates back to that era. From another angle in the yard, I could look toward a thicket of trees where the freedmen's town of Mitchelville once stood. Mary lived on land that was once part of Fish Haul Plantation, the same land that brought sustenance and independence to our family after the war. But the vestiges of all that history were invisible among the ranch homes where Mary lived off Wiley Lane.

Like Phoebe and all living relatives up North, Mary knew nothing about our enslaved ancestors. But it was Mary's immediate family that was more deeply connected to land that relatives and our ancestors inhabited for some 200 years, as well as the culture that sprang from that experience. Mary and her brother Sam and Phoebe's daughter were the ones who lived on land not far from where our ancestors lay.

Mary was deeply dedicated to family. She also grew up on the farm in the Grasslawn section of Hilton Head decades before the bridge to the mainland was constructed, when Gullah-Geechee Creole was spoken everywhere. She knew that Nancy Christopher—the well-known midwife—delivered her in 1935 and that she was a relative. Nancy had been born enslaved at Fish Haul and had been married to Sancho's brother, Murray.[6] She was part of a tradition of midwives who delivered babies during enslavement and passed on their knowledge to the next generation. Nancy successfully brought many of the island's babies into the world. On the island, midwives would prepare expectant mothers, offering prenatal advice. When labor pains began, they would arrive for duty. Midwives would record the dates children were born and remember those they delivered. Island residents generally knew the names of midwives who'd delivered them.[7]

Mary's home was a gathering place. She embraced me as Phoebe did and told me she loved me when I left. Every time I talked with her between 2010 and 2018, relatives were present, either visiting, or living with her for a while: from her daughter, Wanda; her son, Reco; a niece, Amanda, she was close to; and a grandson visiting from Philadelphia.

During my last interview with Mary as she lay back in a recliner, she talked of a childhood filled with good memories. She offered some additional details and impressions of her early life and was straightforward about the resentment she felt toward family members, including her grandmother Sarah (my great-grandmother), who went north and never came South to visit her, her brothers, or her sisters. Because there were no high schools on Hilton Head, she too, like Phoebe, attended school on a nearby coastal island that had one. Mary went to Robert Smalls High School on nearby St. Helena Island. The school was named after a formerly enslaved man who piloted a ship to freedom during the Civil War and went on to serve in the House of Representatives. Mary's marriage at age 19 to Charley Bryant, a marine and professional musician, took her out of the area for decades to Seattle and Tacoma, Washington, and Great Falls, Michigan, before she and Charles settled in Savannah with their five children.

Leaving Hilton Head was what island residents dating back to the post–Civil War era did, including her siblings, Margaret, Romena, Sam, Eugene, Cyrus, and Moses. Although Sam and Eugene lived in New York before returning. Mary told me she was drawn back in the 1970s to the relative peace and tranquility of Hilton Head out of concern that one of her sons might end up with the wrong crowd.

When Mary reflected on her youth, she remembered a way of life that no longer exists. "To me it was beautiful. We had a good life,"

Cousin Mary in her home on Wiley Lane. The street was named after her father Arthur Wiley. Mary's house was on land that was once part of Fish Haul Plantation before becoming farmland owned by Mitchelville residents after the Civil War.

she said, during our last interview. "Our daddy was very on top of things."

Her father, Arthur Wiley, cultivated a beautiful garden near her home decades before her family sold much of the land in the 1970s and built homes, including hers. Mary remembers Arthur planting cotton and beans. Her father fished with a bateau and reels and sometimes threw a cast net to catch fish. Cast-net fishing, where a net is thrown from a boat with weights that pull it to the bottom, is believed to be a form of fishing that our West African ancestors used that continued in the Gullah-Geechee region. The net would be thrown and then pulled back up to the boat with shrimp, crabs, and fish in its folds.

Arthur could also make coiled sweetgrass baskets, Mary recalled. The style of basket weaving in the region is known to have derived in Senegambia and continued during enslavement. Arthur would use the baskets, which are made from sweetgrass, saw palmetto leaves, and pine needles, to hold beans, peas, and eggs.

Mary said her father didn't let her brothers and sisters speak Gullah-Geechee Creole in the house, although they didn't call it Gullah or Geechee back then. He'd say: "You can't get a job speaking like that." Instead, he told them: "Leave that talk in the praise house." But Mary said when you were playing with other children you had to speak the Creole, otherwise you'd get teased.

Mary valued the way children were raised when she was growing up. Serious respect for elders was necessary. "How children were raised then was as different as black and white. You had respect for older people." Talking back and disagreeing with elders wasn't tolerated. The upbringing children received enabled them to function anywhere in the world. Her parents put such a high emphasis on respect within her household that siblings were not allowed to argue. Mary said her brothers and sisters were raised to be close-knit, and faith was a part of life.

When Mary was growing up, people would visit root doctors, like Willie Aiken, who she understood was a relative. People would go to Doctor Aiken for anything from help with arthritis to a virus that wouldn't go away. Aiken's medicine worked. People would use an herb called Everlasting Life as a tonic. Mary remembers the bark from teak trees being used for some medicinal purpose that she could no longer remember.

Mary had some strong feelings about relatives who went North. She felt a sense of loss at not being able to see her grandmother, Sarah. "I feel like there was a split in the family," she said. "My mother would go up there and stay for two weeks." But Aunt Julia's visits weren't returned. "Wouldn't you want to check on your grand-kids?" she said. Mary's father, Arthur, didn't like her mother going up to Harlem for those visits. Despite the tensions, communication among family members was never broken. A few northern relatives would go south for visits, and a few southern relatives would go north. Mary remembers Cousin Timmie, Aunt Julia's niece, who was born in Hilton Head and lived around the corner from my grand-mother in Queens, visiting when Mary was growing up. "She loved to come down and ride horses," said Mary.

Mary remembers her Aunt Aggie, Timmie's mother, coming to Hilton Head when her brother Benjamin died. She said my (great) Aunt Mabel would regularly send money and packages to her mother with items for the children. Despite the hard feelings, she remembers one visit that my grandmother made to Hilton Head after leaving the South, perhaps in the 1980s, and having a pleasant visit, laughing and talking.

It makes sense that with physical distance, emotional distance would arise among family members. I don't have insights into why visits were so rare because those who first migrated—my great-grandmother, grandmother, and two great-aunts—are no longer living. But the physical distance might have made it easier for mis-understandings and differences to linger than if we all lived in the same region and saw each other fairly regularly. The inescapable fact is the need for economic mobility and educational and job opportu-nities drove so many of my relatives, like so many Gullah-Geechee, to be among the millions of African Americans who went north during the Great Migration for similar reasons. I suspect the deci-sion to leave for many felt like the only sensible and practical choice to make. And while the choice to leave worked out for most of the relatives I know of—those with children, grandchildren, and great-grandchildren who are middle class, most with homes and college degrees—leaving for New York City came with a cost.

Many of my great-grandmother's descendants have never seen one another. We don't know one another's names or faces and mostly we know nothing about one another's lives. Leaving left a gulf for future generations that have never been to Hilton Head and don't know of the family's roots. I wonder how different things might be if my grandmother and her sisters went back regularly and took their children, including my mother. What if the generations that didn't grow up there got to go out on boats with relatives to fish in the rivers and creeks and eat crab and seafood gumbo when they went home? What if they learned where my great-grandmother Sarah's farm was and what life was like there? What if they found our ancestors had been there long before the Civil War and began farming this land as freedpeople? What if they learned to speak Creole? What if they learned their Gullah-Geechee ancestors had volunteered to free themselves and were buried there?

CHAPTER 10

Where Religion and Justice Intersect

In South Carolina's Lowcountry, small shacks called praise houses were the central gathering place and foundation for religious expression among the Gullah-Geechee dating back to enslavement.[1] Around 1840, plantation owners began allowing the enslaved to use a meetinghouse for worship as they supported efforts to evangelize in rural communities. And the spaces—devoted to prayer, bible readings, and spirituals—were places where the enslaved could worship on their own. People would be married and baptized in praise houses.[2]

A praise house existed on Fish Haul Plantation during enslavement. A former veteran of the colored infantry, Ansel Holmes, who bought land with Sancho, got married at the praise house there before the Civil War.[3]

The praise houses were places where an African-derived worship style called the ring shout was practiced. Members would engage in call-and-response singing with rhythmic hand clapping, moving in a counterclockwise direction. The shout was a means of maintaining African-derived movement and rhythm in sacred spaces at the end of services.[4] "First described by outsiders in 1845, the stylistic antecedents of the ring shout are indisputably African in origin and proliferated in the Gullah-Geechee religious institution of the praise house."[5]

Praise houses seem to provide spaces where an African sensibility was maintained and transmitted and transferred. "The shout grew in popularity in the study area when slave owners outlawed the use of drums for fear that slaves would use them to communicate between plantations," the authors of the Lowcountry Special Resources Study wrote.[6] These modest structures built by the Gullah-Geechee were the space where their spirituality was expressed for more than a century, well into the mid-twentieth century.

In Hilton Head, praise houses, aligned with an established church, functioned until the island's transformation to a resort and retirement community in the 1950s and '60s, according to those I interviewed. Gullah-Geechee communities in Stoney, Squire Pope, Spanish Wells, and Chaplin were dotted with praise houses. They have been described as one-room wooden buildings with a wood heater in the middle that could seat as many as fifty people along benches that served as pews. Praise-house leaders were primarily men who would lead services and maintain the buildings. People would gather to sing hymns and spirituals, read scripture, and pray on Tuesdays, Thursdays, and Sundays in Hilton Head. Formal services at larger churches were not held weekly because residents couldn't afford to hire a full-time minister. To have sermons from ordained pastors, church congregations would pay a pastor from off-island to come over by boat.[7]

When Cousin Mary was a child in the 1930s and '40s, church services initially took place once every three months. And the praise house is where the family would worship each week. Later, when she was older, she said, services were held monthly before becoming weekly as they are now. Hilton Head did not have pastors from the various Christian denominations who could serve their congregations on an ongoing basis. Another unique aspect of Gullah-Geechee Christianity involved a process called "seeking" that enables children around the time of adolescence to become members of the church. Youth are matched with elders, spiritual parents who guide them through a spiritual journey that involves being separated from daily activities, fasting, and prayer. Children would be led into the woods at night to pray and would later reveal their dreams to their spiritual parents. The spiritual parents would interpret children's dreams and decide when the journey would end, at which time they could become full members of the church.[8]

Manigault, like other scholars, liken seeking among the Gullah-Geechee to African rites of passage. "Belief in the authority and wisdom of elders and spiritual parents, the frequent occurrence of dreams and visions, the entrance of a seeker into the wilderness to 'find God,' and the connections made with ancestors are features of the seeking tradition that parallel African traditional and African-derived religions including Yoruba, Santeria and Vodoun."[9]

Authors of the National Park Service study compared how girls going through the seeking process had to wear a string or white cloth around their heads during the process and sometimes be covered with ashes to initiates of the Sande who would wear white head ties and white clay on their faces. The Sande of the Mende ethnic group in Sierra Leone would be initiated into a secret society and gain knowledge from elders or spiritual parents. When they completed the journey, they'd go through a spiritual wash and be immersed in water, linking them to powerful water spirits of the supernatural world.[10] Similarly, seekers in Gullah-Geechee tradition are immersed in water once their journey is over.

Cousin Phoebe remembers aspects of seeking when she was 13. The current practice of being formally welcomed into the Baptist church involves being given the right hand of fellowship—a practice where members literally extend their right hands to new members as a sign of welcome following weeks of study—but seeking was a much more arduous process.

"You couldn't just give your hand to the pastor," said Phoebe.

"You had to pray and dream." You had a spiritual mother you told your dreams to. You would see her in one of your dreams and your parents would listen to you recount your dreams. Part of what was expected, Phoebe explained, was an acknowledgment in a dream that you had completed the necessary spiritual journey to be baptized. "You probably would have a dream telling you, you were okay," she said. "You would then go before the deacons of the church and they would decide whether you were okay." If they decided you had finished your spiritual journey, then you would be baptized and invited into the church as a full member, probably on the same day. Before going through the seeking process, children had to sit on the back bench in the rear of the praise house and weren't able to lead praise house functions.

Seekers would often maintain relationships with their spiritual mothers for life. Long after the seeking process was complete, Phoebe would listen and talk to her spiritual mother, Nancy Ferguson. Whenever Phoebe was sick, she would always try to visit her spiritual mother. "She would talk about the Lord," Phoebe said, "and try to strengthen my faith." Phoebe maintained a relationship with her spiritual mother until she passed.

I talked with Ruthie Mae White, whose sister married a relative of Phoebe's husband. She had vivid memories of her seeking experience in 1953 to join First Euhaw Baptist Church, some thirty miles away from Hilton Head in Ridgeland, South Carolina.

"You're to stay to yourself, alone," said Ruthie Mae. "At midnight you would go to a praying ground and at 6 am you would pray again day after day. This would go on for some time until a committee of church elders decided you were ready to join the church. On Thursday night at the prayer house, they'd bring you in one by one, to see whether you'd had an experience with the Holy Spirit." Ruthie Mae, like the women Manigault-Bryant interviewed extensively, saw a deceased relative, her oldest sister, while seeking. She remembers praying to see her oldest sister who died in childbirth at age 21. "She lived right down the road from us and we would go there every day and sit there after school," Ruthie Mae said. "She would do our hair. She was like Big Mama. We were very attached to her."

Elijah Heyward III, the former Chief Operating Officer of the International African American Museum, grew up in Beaufort and went through a seeking experience in the 1990s that was transformative though different from what earlier generations experienced. "It wasn't the same experience as my parents had but there were certain practices that were maintained. . . . When you were a kid you didn't think about how powerful it was," he told me in a 2023 interview.[11]

Heyward and his father and grandfather discussed the Gullah-Geechee culture of fishing and making cast nets in the film *After Sherman*.

Heyward told me that although he was a 7-year-old child when he was seeking, the process had a significant impact on his life. He said there was the church mother and a water mother who pulled you from the water during baptism. There were elders giving you the sense that your life and faith mattered deeply. "We had our elders sitting with us, teaching us about the traditions of the church and spiritual practices in a distinctive Gullah way," he told me. "There's no way I can fully describe it. . . . Those situations are so powerful. I was navigating a school with few Black people and going into this distinctly African American experience with elders. And this transcendent portal was opening up and connecting me to God. Going back to school made me realize that I was part of something that's bigger than me. That made me feel very, very special."

Just Law

Another aspect of Gullah-Geechee religious practices is a system of justice for civil and domestic conflicts called "Just Law." Under this system, members of a church or faith community could take grievances to church elders who would mediate the disputes and decide on a resolution. The traditional court system was considered the "White man's law" and "unjust law."[12]

Until the full assimilation of Gullah-Geechee faith with traditional Christian denominations in Hilton Head in the 1960s, church elders settled conflicts for violations of established moral codes through the just law system. The goal of Just Law was to settle conflicts in a just way that would make aggrieved parties whole and restore the guilty party to full membership in the community after compensation was complete.

Just Law could be considered the law of the church. If another member of the church reportedly violated another member's rights, the latter could report the violation to a church leader for review under the covenants for the church of Just Law. If the victim chose to take the matter to "unjust law," or the regular justice system, before seeking redress through Just Law, the church could punish the victim.

The authors of *Gullah Days* described the court process. At a hearing held on a Saturday or Sunday afternoon, a person who felt they were unjustly harmed would make their case. Witnesses would make statements. And church deacons would debate whether the church's moral codes had been violated. If they decided they were, the responsible party would have to make amends and perhaps sit on the back bench of the church alongside children who weren't full members of the church.[13]

The fact the Gullah-Geechee community saw the system they devised as Just Law and the court system as "unjust" seems to be a clear critique of the mainstream justice system, which must have been seen as hostile or indifferent to Black people's interests.

The Just Law system, like praise houses, no longer exists in Hilton Head. Cousin Phoebe remembers it. She said sometimes disputes would end up before Judge Hudson, a member of one of a handful of white families on the island who was a judge in the

Beaufort County court system. Judge Hudson wouldn't take any action, Phoebe recalled, but he would send people to appear before the deacon board, which would decide the punishment.

Generally, the deacon board would require the person who was believed to be guilty of some misdeed to sit in the "back seat," the rear pew of the church, until the board decided the person had done sufficient penance and was ready to fully return to the church community. No serious crimes occurred before the bridge was built in 1956, said Phoebe, when this system of punishment prevailed. The most serious case she remembers involved someone running an illegal bootlegging operation. The matter ended up before the church deacons. "Back then, people were afraid of the deacons," she said. But now, she said, no one fears them.

The Gullah-Geechee system of justice has been compared by scholars to the justice system of the Poro and Sande societies in the Upper Guinea Coast. The Poro and Sande, which were secret societies for males and females, regulated social behavior, intervened in disputes, and punished those found guilty of crimes or who had violated the community's interests. The Poro and Sande had a religious function as well as functions involving justice and reserved "high seats" for a few religious elders.[14] The Just Law system among the Gullah-Geechee dates back to enslavement when people could be punished for violating socioreligious authority and being disloyal to the community of the enslaved.[15]

Throughout West Africa, aggrieved parties can still choose to take civil disputes to a traditional court that operates outside of the legal system developed under colonialism. Under the traditional system, a village chief and his or her court listen to both sides and settle the conflict based on established moral codes. During a trip to Ghana in 2017, I visited an Akan village with this type of traditional system, where the chief and his court preside over civil conflicts.

But today churches in Hilton Head all operate under the conventions of mainstream Christian denominations.

CHAPTER 11

Leaving Geechee Behind

❌

Grandma got up with the chickens.

That's how she referred to her lifestyle of rising early to do morning chores before the orange glow of sunlight filtered through the night sky. She was the first to help me begin to understand what life was like in Hilton Head among the Gullah-Geechee. Despite living almost all her adult life in New York City, the biggest, most metropolitan US city, Grandma considered herself to be a country person. And being a country person meant rising while city folk were still sleeping to get about her list of chores: washing and drying clothes, ironing, dusting, and vacuuming. In the mornings when Grandpa came down to eat, Grandma would have grits cooked and warm, perhaps waffles, sausage and a fried egg ready so he could have a waffle, egg, and sausage sandwich.

Grandma (whose married name was Margaret Ruth Pearson and whose friends and family called Ruth or Ruthy) lived not far from the two-family house where I grew up. Hers was a single-family home in St. Albans, Queens that she and my step-grandfather bought in 1950 in a lower middle-class community that had become integrated with Black families before becoming all Black. She had all the modern conveniences of the time: air conditioners, dishwashers, a refrigerator, stove and oven in her kitchen and a small kitchen in the basement apartment downstairs that they kept rented. Her home was a world away from her life as a child on Hilton Head Island where her family farmed off the waters of Port Royal Sound.

When Grandma was born in 1917 and for decades afterward, no town or local government existed on the island. It was virtually all Black and undeveloped. Hilton Head was then a Gullah-Geechee island where people built their own homes and had small farms where they grew crops and raised livestock. People used horse-drawn wagons to travel on unpaved roads and lived without electricity, gas or indoor plumbing. But as my grandmother's niece, Phoebe, pointed out, people ate "straight from the farm and straight from the river." When Grandma shared stories about life growing up on Hilton Head, she would tell me about how Bessie the cow would chase her older sister, Mabel, whenever she saw her. And there was a story about the time when Mabel was bitten by a snake, suffered a seizure, and was unable to open her mouth. Mabel had to see a root doctor, Grandma said. And whatever herbs she was given worked.

Grandma told me her mother had a nursery for a while where she would teach small children and once had a store. But she couldn't keep the store open and profitable because some in the community had little and would ask for food, perhaps milk for the baby, and she would offer it and they wouldn't be able to pay her back.

There were no theaters in Hilton Head when Grandma was growing up. So the church provided one of the only sources of entertainment. On Saturdays, her family would prepare for church and load up the wagon with food because on Sunday they would travel to three churches and would eat in between services. People didn't sing gospel songs, just spirituals. "Let me see if I can remember," she once said. And then she began singing a spiritual song a second later, rhythmically clapping along. The churches didn't have pianos. Back then, she said men could go into the woods and make instruments from trees. She remembered older people speaking a language that wasn't Gullah that she couldn't understand, which makes me wonder whether she heard survivors of enslavement, perhaps born in Africa, who still spoke the languages of their birthplaces. Grandma didn't learn anything about enslavement from anyone, not her mother who had been married to an enslaved man or her grandmother Molly. She was told that Black people in Hilton Head had never lived in enslavement: when the ships carrying captives came to harbor, there were strong swimmers who swam off to safety and made a life for themselves on the island.

When Grandma was five, the family began splitting time between Hilton Head and Savannah, farming in Hilton Head during the warm weather months and back in Savannah during the winter. Earning enough money to survive had to have been challenging. Moses Polite was about 30 years older than my great-grandmother and when he died in 1907, she was 33 years old with Aggie, Clarence, and Julia to raise at the time. So for a couple of decades, the family worked in Savannah for extended periods of time while maintaining the farm in Hilton Head. When Grandma was 12 her mother and siblings began staying in Savannah year-round. And because the city had high schools, she was the first of her siblings to graduate high school. About a decade later, she would leave the area for good.

Grandma was the type of girl who should never live in the South, people said, because she was too defiant and outspoken. She was not willing to wear the mask of subservience required of Black people in the Jim Crow era. One time while doing domestic work as a teenager in a white family's house in Savannah, she had to run out of the house when someone "tried something," which I assume was an attempt at sexual assault. Grandma also told me of a physical confrontation with a white man that could have gotten her killed or run out of town in some places in the South: A white man they had never seen came to the family's home and began yelling at her mother, insisting that she pay him money he claimed she owed. From time to time, Grandma said, white people would come into Black communities and harass people with some scheme to get money. But Grandma wouldn't stand for it. She grabbed the man by the scruff of his neck, pushed him up against a wall, and told him to get out of the area, warning him to never come back. Clearly, such defiance was incredibly risky. The oppressiveness of Jim Crow may have given her another reason to leave the segregated South with its rigidly defined caste system.

Grandma, Margaret Ruth Pearson, around the time of her marriage to my grandfather Jack.

After high school, Grandma married James "Jack" White, of Jacksonville, Florida. And at 19, she gave birth to my mother, Shirley Ruth White. I never talked with my grandmother about her life in Savannah as a young adult when my mother was an infant. Cousin Phoebe remembers when family members went north in 1938 or 1939. She thinks my grandmother's sister, Mabel, and great-grandmother went first. And my grandparents left Savannah for Washington, DC, with my mother when Jack got a good job on a loading dock there and an opportunity to go to school at night. Phoebe said she had to go back to Hilton Head to live with her parents on the farm.

My grandfather James "Jack" White.

Grandma in the summer of 1939 with my mother at age 2, her oldest sister Aunt Aggie and Aggie's son Vincent. This picture was taken at the World's Fair in New York City about the time she moved to Harlem.

During the Great Migration, from 1916 to 1970, nearly half of the Black Southerners, about six million people, left for higher paying jobs, often in factories, and a less rigid racial caste system, seeking lives free of the terrorism they'd known. Aunt Mabel and my great-grandmother headed to Harlem and were joined by Aunt Aggie, the oldest of my grandmother's siblings.

When I think of the impetus to migrate among my relatives something Murray, my distant cousin, said to me seems relevant. When he was growing up, anyone with an "ounce of ambition" didn't want to stay in Hilton Head. Most everyone growing up there wanted to leave. While many found better economic opportunities, there were downsides. Northern racism still imposed limitations. And while there was some degree of tension among some, mostly the generations born in the North and future generations born in the South in my family became strangers. And those raised up North became disconnected from the Gullah-Geechee culture and family's heritage there.

Grandma's first stop on the journey North to Washington, DC, would be brief—perhaps not more than a year. One day my grandfather Jack came home from his job on a loading dock, told my grandmother he didn't feel well, and said he needed to lie down. He fell asleep and never woke up. His co-workers told my grandmother that he got hurt when a truck backed into him at the loading dock, probably causing him to die of internal injuries.

Although Grandma would occasionally mention Jack's name, she never talked to me about the pain she must have gone through and how his death affected her life. My mom was too young to remember him. But she knew her mother adored him, and she'd send her South on the train to Jacksonville, Florida to visit his family when she was older.

After Jack died Grandma remained in the North and moved in with her mother and Aunt Mabel in Harlem, New York. It was about 1939. Everyone lived at a Harlem apartment on 112 Bradhurst Avenue near 155th Street. Until my mother was 12, she lived in an extended family arrangement there as well with her grandmother Sarah, aunts, nieces, and a nephew. The Bradhurst Avenue apartment, according to my cousin Eileen who grew up in Harlem, was the first stop for relatives when they arrived in New York from Hilton Head or Savannah. People would stay there until they were settled in a job and found their own place.

Grandma, like her sisters, Mabel and Aggie, initially did domestic work. But Grandma would later work in a factory as a seamstress making hats for infants. She was a member of the International Ladies Garment Workers Union. Years later, she worked as a clerical worker for the Nurse's Registry on 57th Street in Manhattan, where she was a member of the Service Employees International Union 1199. Grandma had gone from life as a child where land was a few dollars an acre, to working in Manhattan just a couple blocks south of Central Park, an area with some of the priciest real estate in the country.

When Grandma was in her 20s, money was tight. She spent a brief time on public assistance before she married Cecil Pearson, the man I knew as my grandfather. Grandma always worked and mom never went hungry but remembers a few times when dinner consisted of nothing but cream of wheat. The neighborhood on 155th Street and Bradhurst Avenue was tough. My mother remembered gangs in the neighborhood and someone firing a zip gun, a home-made gun fashioned out of a pipe, in the stairwell. Grandma made my mother stand up to a neighborhood bully once, ordering her to go outside and fight the girl or she'd have to come back inside to fight her. Cousin Kitty came by with friends to make sure Mom stood up to the bully and won the fight.

But aside from that, I mostly heard of the good times living in Harlem. Harlem is where my mother's dream to become a dancer was born. Grandma talked occasionally about memories of Harlem's famous Savoy Ballroom, known for great Lindy Hoppers, where Ella Fitzgerald and Count Basie's band played. Once she started dancing in my living room in Queens trying to recall steps to the Lindy Hop. Old black-and-white photographs show Grandma and relatives in Harlem in satin dresses and fur stoles. Grandma remembered Malcolm X, then known as Detroit Red, who frequented the Savoy, walking into bars in Harlem with an entourage of light-skinned Black women. It was around that time that he briefly dated her niece, Timmie.

Grandma would not spend many years of her life in Harlem. She married Cecil and a few years later they bought a house in St. Albans, Queens—a 10-minute drive from the house I grew up in. When Grandma moved to Queens with my mother and grandpa, my great-grandmother moved with them. Grandpa worked as a porter at AT&T for decades and was a World War II army veteran.

My mother began middle school in Queens continuing to take dance classes outside of school. After graduating high school, she attended The Juilliard School where she majored in dance. My mother's passion for dance ignited at age 7 or 8 when a family friend took her to Radio City Music Hall, and she saw a professional ballet performance. When she returned home, eyes wide with excitement, she told her mother and grandmother that she wanted to be a dancer just like the women she saw performing. My great-grandmother, Sarah, told her she'd give her a nickel to pay for classes each week— even though she'd never heard of a colored girl making a living as a dancer.

Mom became a modern dancer and spent her performing career dancing with several professional modern dance companies, touring the United States and even traveling to perform in Africa, the Middle East, and Europe. She taught dance for decades and choreographed for her own company, Rushing-Danz Inc. A highlight of her career was performing with hundreds of dancers in the movie version of

(*From left to right standing*) Aunt Mabel, cousin Berniece (Clarence's daughter), my grandmother, Ruth at her home in Queens. (*Seated*) My grandmother's brother Clarence, my great-grandmother Sarah Polite and Cousin Timmie.

SHIRLEY RUSHING

One of my mother's promotional dance photos. On the upper right, during a break in filming *The Wiz*, she is seated next to Michael Jackson dressed as the Scarecrow.

The Wiz. While teaching dance in Guadalupe, she choreographed a piece for a soloist with the Paris Opera Ballet, who was also a visiting teacher and the soloist performed it with that ballet company in France. As a dance professor at Spelman College in Atlanta when I was a toddler, she taught Samuel L. Jackson while he was a student at Morehouse. Coretta Scott King would bring her daughter, Yolanda, to dance classes on weekends and so would the parents of actress Jasmine Guy. Back in New York, Mom briefly taught the actor Denzel Washington while he was in college.

The life Grandma made in New York and the opportunities she was able to offer my mother were unimaginable in Hilton Head and less likely to have happened even in Savannah. Grandma said she always encouraged mom to pursue her passion for dance, a passion she shared. And my Great-Grandmother Sarah, Sancho's daughter, born not long after the Civil War ended, supported a dream she couldn't even envision because it was my mother's dream. Clearly, she understood that a Black girl's dreams needed to be supported if they were ever to come true. Because of the circumstances of her life in Hilton Head and Savannah, Grandma's dreams were by necessity more pragmatic than my mother's dreams. She had to improve the material condition of her life outside the South to offer her daughter opportunities that were unavailable to her.

Grandma was hardworking, disciplined, patient, and focused. She could account for every penny she'd spent. And years of paid bills were paperclipped and boxed in case she ever needed to prove she paid them. She maintained a Christmas club, along with regular savings, and checking accounts. Grandma would use a credit card for convenience but would never carry a balance. Before my grandparents bought the house in Queens, Grandpa wanted to use his wartime earnings to buy a new car. But Grandma insisted they buy a house. She made sure a good portion of Grandpa's earnings from his job as a porter at AT&T, which he affectionately called Mama Bell, was used to buy company stock, which eventually grew to hundreds of thousands of dollars in retirement.

Grandma was able to help pay for my school clothes and assist with private school tuition, which helped because we were living on a dancer's income and my father's earnings as an adjunct professor who also drove a cab and worked in retail while pursuing his doctoral degree. Grandma had achieved the American dream through her hard work, ambition, and gumption. For years, she was a hairdresser on the side on weekends while working full time during the week. Grandpa took side jobs doing home repairs. They usually kept the small basement apartment in their home rented.

Grandma had little use for TV. One source of entertainment was the holiday family dinner. She'd set the table the day before with the good china, the silverware polished to a shine, and starched white tablecloths. She'd prep her food in advance. And at the dinners—

typically Thanksgiving, Christmas, or Easter—food was served on time, with meat and gravy and dinner rolls served hot.

Grandma, like my mother, was very composed and dignified. She never seemed frazzled and always seemed to have it together. I never heard her raise her voice. She wasn't a churchgoer, but faith was always part of her life. Any plans or hopes for the future were placed "in the hands of the good Lord."

Like other Hilton Head residents, Grandma didn't talk about identifying as Geechee or Gullah. But she lived with the stigma that coming from Hilton Head carried. When my mother was growing up, Grandma told her not to tell anyone the family was from Hilton Head. "Just tell them we're from Savannah," she'd say. "They'll call you a Geechee if you tell them you're from Hilton Head."

On Grandma's first trip back to the island since she had left in the 1930s, she found it beautiful. But by the 1980s, it did not look like the farming and fishing communities with dirt roads she knew growing up; the island of her childhood was gone. Nevertheless, she still was careful to obey Gullah-Geechee cultural norms. On that trip when people mistook her for her older sister Aggie, she said she avoided explaining because she knew not to correct old people. Doing so would have been rude. She believed in adhering to the cultural expectations she learned by not doing what any typical American or even African American would do, which is to immediately clear up any confusion about who she was. It was more important that the elders not feel any embarrassment from being corrected than it was for her to explain. The reverence for elders was what mattered.

I don't know if she thought much about her identity as a young adult, since being Gullah or Geechee was not discussed. And I don't know what she might have thought about Hilton Head in her early years and when she returned as an elder. Perhaps she thought more about what she would have lacked living there. But in her old age, she showed she identified with the African heritage, she learned about as a child. When I was in my 20s, a friend from graduate school who grew up in Nigeria would come over for dinners during the holidays. On one of those occasions, when we sat around the table talking, she glanced over at my friend and said: "We always knew we were African. And when I see him, I see it. And now I know what they told us was true." Something about his mannerisms and style of speaking must have reminded her of the adults she grew up around.

History mattered to my grandmother. She kept four silver dollars from the 1870s. I have them now. They likely belonged to Sancho or Molly or other relatives of their generation since my great-grandmother would have been a very young child at the time. Grandma kept Moses Polite's original Civil War discharge papers, dated April 35, 1866. The form with words filled out in cursive is so old that the scotch tape used to hold it together has dissolved into the form. Grandma also kept her mother's marriage certificate to Moses from 1896. The marriage certificate is so delicate that I'm afraid that it would fall apart if I attempt to unfold it.

CHAPTER 12

The Double-Edged Sword

While African aspects of Gullah-Geechee culture, like names that come from specific ethnicities and languages, are clear markers of African heritage and cultural retention, a more obscure aspect of African heritage within the culture is evident in the Gullah-Geechee sense of land ownership.

Scholars have focused little attention on African-derived concepts of kinship, family structure, and codes of behavior among the Gullah-Geechee, according to Bamidele Agbasegbe Demerson, who explored how the Gullah-Geechee in the Sea Islands traditionally lived in family compounds with three generations of families living in adjacent clusters on the same property—similar to how families have lived in West Africa. Land was owned by extended families and, sometimes, still is, passed down based on bloodlines and relationships to a common ancestor.[1] "Given that slavery would have rendered inoperative the function of lineages, it is particularly interesting to observe that after slavery, some of the corporate functions of African lineages reemerged in some extended families which became property-owning collectives," Demerson wrote.[2]

Murray Christopher, the cousin I found through this research, who first took me to Sancho's gravesite, is descended from a long line of male Christophers, including my great-great grandfather's brother Murray whose name was passed down to him. Although the island is vastly different from the Hilton Head Murray grew up on, what remains unchanged is that the land where he lives is still a kinship-based family compound. Murray's family compound is not uncommon among Gullah-Geechee in Hilton Head—although they may not be visible to outsiders.

When I visited Murray in 2018, I pulled off the island's fast-moving main corridor, William Hilton Parkway, to drive to his home on Christopher Drive. I first passed a few small houses where his nieces and nephews live with their children on family land that their ancestors farmed since at least the 1880s, he told me. When Murray thinks about the value of Gullah-Geechee culture, he thinks of the way extended families lived together. "You had this concept like an African village, a family compound with parents, grandparents, sisters, and brothers all living in one area," he said. "You had multigenerational families living together. People would build homes close by, next door, right across the way." The land has been central to the survival of Gullah-Geechee culture, he told me. "The connection to the land for me is the most important aspect of the culture," Murray said. "It's almost spiritual."

Land, where our ancestors once labored when enslaved, historically represented liberation and self-sufficiency, Murray told me. His parents and siblings fished and farmed like other Gullah-Geechee families. They grew watermelon, peas, beans, corn, sweet potatoes, and okra and would take some of it to Savannah to sell. Murray's family fished just about every day, catching shrimp, fish, and crabs from wooden bateaus with cast nets they made. Although casting is mostly associated with men, Murray said women went casting too. His mom was proficient at throwing a cast net. After fish were caught, women would sometimes get together, clean the fish, and dry it out in the sun to preserve it.[3]

In addition to family compounds, another African-derived concept among the Gullah-Geechee involved how ownership and land usage were determined. Throughout much of West Africa, one's lineage—whether a group utilizes a matrilineal or patrilineal system—determines one's obligations and one's rights. Belonging to a certain lineage could determine whether one gained access to inherited land. Lineage could also help define whether you could succeed to political or religious offices allocated to a particular descent group or whether you could acquire training or an occupation practiced by members of the group.[4] A similar approach to land ownership and use also survived the transatlantic slave trade among the Gullah-Geechee and the people of Haiti and Suriname, among African descendants of maroon communities formed by those who escaped enslavement.[5]

The form of land ownership and connection to land was not only linked to the Gullah-Geechee's West African heritage but also the circumstances surrounding the Civil War. Demerson wrote: "Of particular significance were the federal occupation of the Sea Islands, the liberation of enslaved Africans, and the land redistribution scheme (albeit precarious) that occurred during the Civil War. The Freedmen's Bureau, the Direct Tax Act of 1861, and the South Carolina Land Commission provided avenues through which an ex-bondsman could become a landholder of the estate (or portion thereof) on which Africans and their descendants were once enslaved."[6]

The Gullah-Geechee define "family" with respect to land ownership in a much more inclusive way than most Americans. Their concept of family was built around ties to a common ancestor while the typical concept in America is family built around a conjugal bond. When couples marry in typical American families, they generally establish a home away from their families of origin. And the focus is the nuclear family. In contrast, in Gullah-Geechee families, men were generally seen as the heads of households. When men got married, they were expected to bring their wives to their family compound and build a house near other male relatives who were heads of their own households on the same or adjacent property.[7]

Although ownership was conferred largely through male lineage, women who inherited their husband's or parents' land in Hilton Head would often serve as matriarchs, playing a leading role in deciding how the land on Hilton Head was used.

"It was always a patriarch or matriarch who would point out how land was to be used by the family based on lineage," said Campbell. What you were entitled to use was in part determined by your position in the line of descent. The Gullah-Geechee took a collaborative approach to land management. As the eldest of his siblings, Campbell's father would hold court every month with his brothers and sisters. At the meetings, they would discuss how the family would use the land and how land taxes would be paid. Campbell's family's taxes were paid through pecan sales. And Campbell remembers bagging many bags of pecans as a child.

The Gullah-Geechee concept of land ownership aligns with how the Igbo of Nigeria saw it, wrote Michael Gomez, a professor at New York University, who researched the cultural influence of ethnic groups in Africa on African Americans. "Land was ultimately owned by the lineage, not the individual," he wrote of the Igbo of Nigeria. "It was the responsibility of the *okpara,* or lineage head, to oversee the equitable distribution of lineage or communal land."[8]

When I visited Cousin Mary in her home, her niece (Phoebe's daughter) was right next door. And Mary's and Phoebe's brother, Sam, lived right down the road on Wiley Lane. When Phoebe, Mary, Sam, and their siblings subdivided the land in the 1970s and sold most of it to a land developer, who began selling lots for homes, they still shared a space tied to a common ancestor. In this case, their father had purchased the land. Like Campbell's family, they had homes within yards of one another. This level of physical closeness provides a stark contrast to many families I know in Washington, DC, who dread lengthy visits with their parents, the grandparents to their children, and prefer to live many states away from them.

The Gullah-Geechee concept of shared ownership among de-

The Double-Edged Sword / 169

scendants was the only reason Phoebe's brother Gene told my parents that they should build a house on land that belonged to my great-grandmother. Our shared lineage made my mother and me, like him, rightful owners. No will was needed to claim ownership. Unfortunately, my father had no means to even consider building a second home at that point in his life.

My grandmother also thought of her mother's land as the property of all her mother's descendants. She told me when I was a young adult that the family owned twenty-two acres of land in Mitchelville and that her share would pass on to me and my mother. Grandma also told me the family had pinelands at one time as well as beachfront property. And she remembered a time, growing up, when all the men in the family got together in a room to discuss selling land. She doesn't know what decision they made because she was too young for anyone to discuss it with her. But her concept of land ownership passing on to me and my mother was typical for the Gullah-Geechee in Hilton Head.

When I talked with Emory about land ownership in Hilton Head, he said the Gullah-Geechee concept of land ownership and decision making was almost like a village in West Africa where the chief is in charge. "And, in our case, sometimes the chief was a lady," he said. Although Demerson said land ownership was generally tied to descent from males in the Sea Islands, Campbell said ownership in Hilton Head could be linked to a male or female owner, based on the circumstances.

One can understand the unifying bonds linked to generational land, but the Gullah-Geechee approach to land ownership, which did not involve the use of wills, left it legally vulnerable to unscrupulous relatives and developers. Under heirs' property laws, one heir can force land to be sold to a prospective buyer even when other heirs don't want to sell. The legal system in South Carolina, like other states, privileges an individual's ability to sell heirs' property over the rest of the heir's descendants.

In recent decades when land values in Hilton Head skyrocketed, a land rush began, tension and division grew among family members, and the level of family cohesion that was common among Gullah-Geechee began eroding over land squabbles about whether to sell the land, according to Campbell and others I interviewed.

Property issues among heirs contributed to the transformation of Hilton Head from a nearly all-Black Gullah-Geechee island to one in which they are only a small minority. But the transition should be understood within the context of a lack of infrastructure, political power, and socioeconomic progress, shaped by the same invisible white hands that had set up a Jim Crow system that depended on the marginalization and subjugation of Black people throughout South Carolina. The wealth and power disparity between the relatively small number of Gullah-Geechee who had been there for centuries and the tens of thousands of wealthy that would move in made a massive transformation inevitable. But the changes could have happened in a far more inclusive way.

As Campbell pointed out, the white power structure "never did anything" for island residents, even though they'd been paying taxes on the land since their ancestors were freed. Electricity and indoor plumbing weren't available on the island until the 1950s when developers believed they could exploit the island for profit. But decades before any of that happened, people were leaving Hilton Head, as census data shows, seemingly pushed out by the limited cash economy, educational opportunities or social progress. The desire to have a steady source of income, a home, whether rented or owned, with central heat, running water, and electricity surely must have been the magnet pulling people to the mainland. In the 1930s, for example, when Phoebe was in elementary school and living with my grandmother and great-grandmother in Savannah, she specifically mentioned their apartment had electricity, running water, and a bathroom.[9]

But leaving Hilton Head was a double-edged sword. On the one hand, land meant independence and freedom and not facing the daily humiliation of Jim Crow and racial trauma. It meant not having to depend on white people for your livelihood. But the freedom, autonomy, and sense of community of Hilton Head meant sacrificing economic growth and the modern conveniences people had on the mainland.

If you look back across centuries to the immediate aftermath of enslavement, the possibility of a far more equitable society looked promising. Black people received full citizenship under federal law when Congress passed the Civil Rights Act of 1866. The Reconstruction Acts of 1867 granted voting rights to Black men and weakened the political power of former Confederate states. The law also forced military rule on the former Confederate states and required that states seeking readmission to the union ratify the Fourteenth Amendment, which offered full citizenship rights to African Americans. In some areas of the South, 90 percent of eligible Black voters voted. It might have appeared to those freed, initially, that equality was at hand for a few years. State legislatures saw an infusion of more than 600 newly Black elected representatives. Black voters made a huge impact on discriminatory laws after receiving the right to vote in 1867 when reconstruction acts were passed. Black elected officials in Southern states repealed vagrancy laws, which were used to force Black men into involuntary servitude for loitering or being unemployed. They made corporal punishment illegal and restricted the number of capital offenses.

In 1868, the majority of state representatives elected to South Carolina were Black. It is likely that Sancho and his brothers-in-law, Adam and Jacob Jenkins, who became registered voters along with the thousands of newly freed voters from Beaufort County, helped elect them. There were seven times as many Black voters as white voters, which led to multiple representatives from Beaufort being elected to the statehouse. The well-known Robert Smalls, who was formerly enslaved and was able to pilot a boat to free himself during the Civil War, was elected to Congress numerous times. Beaufort County stood out for Black representation in its national, state, and local offices; city council; board of education; magistrates; coroners; and sheriffs. Among those elected as a county commissioner and coroner was Renty Greaves, who had been enslaved in Bluffton and came to Hilton Head right after the Battle of Port Royal. Sancho knew Greaves. They were witnesses for each other's disability pension claims after the Civil War.

Grappling with Political and Economic Disenfranchisement

But as Black people asserted political power and allied with white Republicans, they faced an increasing reign of terror throughout the South from white Democrats at all levels of society: from former Confederate officers and enslavers to lawyers and ministers. By the 1868 election, white southerners formed paramilitary organizations to reassert white supremacy and stifle Black political power. Groups like the Ku Klux Klan, the Knights of the White Camelia, the Pale Faces, and the Red Shirts began targeting and terrorizing African Americans. The terror Black people faced, including whippings and lynchings, happened without any accountability for the atrocious attacks. Some 400 incidents of lynching in the South are believed to have occurred between 1868 and 1871.[10]

In 1872, the possibility of greater equity for the newly emancipated was gutted by a Supreme Court decision that restricted the scope of the Fourteenth Amendment to citizenship rights, leaving enforcement of voting rights in the South to state courts, which had no concerns about protecting the franchise for Black people. To make things worse, Congress passed an amnesty bill returning full civil rights to Confederates along with eligibility to hold public office.[11]

In 1878, Black voters in Beaufort would face political violence from a white supremacist group, the Red Shirts, and take up arms to defend themselves. The incident happened in Gillisonville, then the seat of Beaufort County, when Representative Robert Smalls was about to deliver a campaign speech as he sought reelection to Congress. Some 800 Red Shirts, led by former Confederate officers, swarmed the storefront where Smalls was planning to speak. The Confederates began knocking the hats off Black men and slapping Black women. A former Confederate colonel demanded to speak to the gathering, but Smalls told him the meeting was canceled and went into a store with forty of his associates. The men with Smalls were armed and ready to fire if any Red Shirts entered. Word spread quickly in the majority Black county and some 1,000 people began approaching with guns, axes, and hoes, prompting most of the Red Shirts to leave. About twenty Red Shirts stayed behind, however, seeking to apprehend Smalls, but he managed to escape.[12]

As white southerners gained more political power, South Carolina, like other Southern states, almost completely disenfranchised Black voters through poll taxes and literacy tests in the 1890s.[13] Despite the political disenfranchisement that eliminated the ability of Black voters to pass laws and control resources, Hilton Head's Gullah-Geechee community continued their lives, fishing and farming and earning money in the ways they could—or leaving when these means were no longer working out.

Families in the various Hilton Head communities owned plots of land varying in size from 25 acres to 60 acres. Some owned small businesses, convenience stores, and restaurants. One of the most well-known entrepreneurs was Charlie Simmons Sr., who owned a store, nicknamed Big Star, that opened in the 1940s in the Stoney section of Hilton Head. It sold everything from blue jeans, socks, and underwear to stoves, lantern oil, rice, and turpentine. People thought of Stoney as a mini-downtown because it had several shops with items you otherwise couldn't get unless you went off-island to

Savannah. Simmons operated numerous boats and eventually began running a gas-powered ferry that took people to Savannah with a stop in Daufuskie, the closest island to Hilton Head. James Frazier owned a blacksmith shop in the Jonesville section of the island, where he made anchors for boats and wagon wheels. (Horse-drawn wagons were the main method of transportation through the mid-1950s.) Daniel Frazier, a relative of James Frazier, was a well-known carpenter who would build homes that were higher than most with porches. Members of the Green Family, considered the best boat builders on the island, would sell their sailboats to families all over the island. The Christophers in the Chaplin section of the island were known for the cast nets they made.[14]

And there were industrious men like Ben White Sr., an expert farmer, who owned a tractor when few others did. He would turn and till soil for anyone who needed it. He owned multiple plots of land and leased some of it to expand the amount of vegetables he could sell at the market in Savannah. While he was in Savannah, his workers would ship fresh produce to him using Charlie Simmons ferry if some produce was running low. White sent fifteen of his seventeen children to college. He was a fierce advocate for education and served on the Southern Beaufort County Board of Education.[15]

Singleton Beach, Burke's Beach, and Bradley Beach continued to cater to Black families when the island began gentrifying. Black professionals, physicians, and college professors from Savannah invested in vacation homes near Burke's Beach and Bradley Beach before desegregation in the 1960s. Juke joints, where people could listen to music and dance, operated near beaches and in the communities around the island. Across from Driessen Beach, land that Phoebe and her husband Henry sold to the city, was a large pavilion for concerts, an arcade building, and a Black-owned motel, Campbell told me. But, with the passage of the Civil Rights Act of 1964, beaches and entertainment venues that had excluded Black folks in Savannah and other cities around the South desegregated and the

Hilton Head businesses that catered to middle-class African Americans were no longer viable.

Black businesses began to struggle on Hilton Head amid massive investment from white-run development companies and corporations that were radically transforming island life. The Black population did not get to have much if any say in the island's future. "The social structure would've had to be different for Black people to have played more of a role in the development," said Campbell. "You would've had to have better educational opportunities, a better economic system to be able to borrow money from a bank."

The disenfranchisement of Black people put them at a tremendous disadvantage. While the Gullah-Geechee welcomed the bridge and eagerly anticipated the first electric lines that arrived in 1951, considering it necessary progress, they didn't know then that white people from outside the island would attempt to change their way of life.

Hilton Head could be a very different place today if those developing resorts had reached out to those who had lived there for countless generations to plan and even bring them on as owners. What if those whose families navigated the waterways for a couple of centuries to catch fish, clams, oysters and crab, were tour guides who could tell visitors about the wildlife, creeks, tidal wetlands, and fishing methods? What if those who were great cooks with knowledge of the Gullah-Geechee cuisine and foodways were creating menus for the new restaurants that would be opened? But that's conjecture about a far more equitable society than the one we live in. Exclusion and marginalization have been the norm.

One aspect of the development that has been particularly offensive to descendants of the enslaved has been naming resorts and housing developments after plantations. "Charles Fraser and them (the developers) were shrewd enough to know that northerners wanted to live like plantation owners," said Campbell. Although the common perception is that white northerners were opposed to enslavement, Fraser knew they could market the fantasy of a return to the opulent lifestyle of the Old South while ignoring the complete exploitation of Black people who lived lives confined to laboring on those plantations. After Sea Pines opened, other planned communities sprang up over the next few decades using the names of plantations that once existed on the island.

Despite decades of complaints and a recent coordinated campaign following Black Lives Matter protests in the summer of 2020, the 4,000-acre Hilton Head Plantation still uses the term "plantation" in the name of its properties. Some 10,000 people live there, its website indicated on April 17, 2024. The Hilton Head Plantation Property Owners' Association publishes a monthly newsletter called Plantation Living. The idea that plantation living is something positive and celebratory completely ignores the reality of the forced labor, rapes, whippings, and breaking up of families that the enslaved experienced at the hands of white enslavers. The name manifests profound erasure and dehumanization of Hilton Head's Gullah-Geechee ancestors who labored and struggled to survive on the land these resort communities now occupy.

Sea Pines, the first resort and retirement community on Hilton Head, dropped "plantation" from its name and added resort after coming under pressure, including Campbell's criticism of the use of "plantation" during an appearance on the news program *60 Minutes*. Sea Pines' owners still, however, hang on to the name Sea Pines' Plantation Golf Club.

In addition to the plantation names, the locked gates, Campbell said, also show a major disconnect, sending a message that Black folks are not welcome unless entering to clean or perform some type of service job. He explained that such an approach to development could only happen when Black voices were not involved in decision making. "Even today," Campbell says, "Black people are seen as a hindrance to progress."

The feeling of being marginalized and outside the power structure continues to resonate for many Gullah-Geechee on Hilton Head Island. In the summer of 2021, the South Carolina Department of Transportation proposed widening the island's main thoroughfare, William Hilton Parkway, which would displace Black-owned business and swallow up property that had been in Gullah-Geechee families for generations.[16]

The Town of Hilton Head's lone Black council member, Alex Brown, who's also Gullah-Geechee, is concerned that those who oppose the widening of William Hilton Parkway may be unable to stop it. I interviewed Brown, and he said the idea of native islanders losing property along that route feels like another "slap in the face." He described what the Gullah-Geechee community is experiencing with respect to land ownership as being like "death by a thousand cuts."[17] (Brown's great-great grandfather, Prince Brown, knew my ancestors. Adam Jenkins and Murray Christoper who served with him in the 21st regiment were witnesses for his wife's pension benefits.)

Ward 1, which Brown represents, is home to the largest percentage of Gullah-Geechee residents, according to the *Greenville News*. "When they first built the bridge, it bisected that community. Then they went from two lanes to four lanes, taking more of it," he told me. Brown wants those angered by the proposal to advocate for a solution that would help repair the damage that development has caused to Black communities. He opposes the expansion of William Hilton Parkway, but if it's going to go forward, he'd like to consider trading off the loss of some property with some land in Stoney, the area where Hilton Head's mini downtown with Gullah-Geechee-owned businesses was based before the bridge was built. The town acquired that land bit by bit from Black families, much of it heirs' property, and has left it largely vacant for reasons that are rooted in racism, he says. "It was purchased with the intent of getting rid of the Black people on the main strip," he said.

But now, with a greater understanding of the importance of preserving Gullah-Geechee culture, native islanders have enough political capital to raise the town's harmful erasure of Stoney and call for a restoration of the area as a Gullah-Geechee community, he told me. Land that might be taken under the right of eminent domain for the road expansion could be replaced in Stoney. "Now we have this different platform of preservation," he said. "Let's come up with a development plan. Let's let our visitors see this proudful mixed use Gullah area."

St. James Baptist Church, my family's church, has roots in historic Mitchelville, and it is now being forced to move because Hilton Head Airport expanded, adding a new terminal and longer runway. The church, founded by freedpeople in the 1880s, is being displaced by Beaufort County officials to accommodate more and larger planes to serve upper income travelers. Once again, the Gullah-Geechee community's interests are being swept aside for perceived growth and progress.[18]

Decades of gentrification have made Hilton Head's Black residents a small minority, comprising just 6 percent of the population, or 2,300 of the island's 40,000 full-time residents, according to a 2019 census data.[19] Eighty percent of the island's land is now inside private communities. The Gullah-Geechee in Hilton Head have not left, and the population has not decreased in recent decades. The island's total population, when it was almost all Black, was around 1,000 in 1951 when electricity came to Hilton Head. And now the Black population has more than doubled. But Hilton Head's Gullah-Geechee community has been enveloped by more and more people who come from elsewhere, and most of the land they owned has been lost or sold. The Gullah-Geechee now own 1,000 acres or 8 percent of the island's residential land. The land owned by Black people has decreased by 70 percent since 1995, and the overall population has increased by 70 percent.[20]

Many Gullah-Geechee residents sold farmland, tree-covered

plots, and beachfront land in the northern part of Hilton Head that is now home to condominiums, residential housing tracts, and hotels. One of the island's Black beaches, Singleton Beach, was technically owned by the Singleton family but all had access. That beach has been privatized and the only people with access are the owners of private oceanfront townhomes.

In 2010, on my first trip there, I walked with my cousin Eileen toward the beach, and her jaw dropped when she realized that the quiet beach which she used to walk to from her grandmother's house was gone. She was shocked that the Singletons had sold it. I ventured over to look at the beach, walking past the private, colorful town-homes and luxury vehicles parked outside, trespassing to look at it. A sign warned me that I was entering private property. I felt that I should make the stop brief out of concern that I could be stopped and questioned for violating the law.

The gentrification of Hilton Head was inevitable given the amount of land Fraser and Hack could easily acquire and the interest in vacationing or retiring along the beachfront among wealthier outsiders. But it also happened to some extent with the unintentional help of Gullah-Geechee residents. Those who didn't see a need for old farmland, woods, or beachfront but saw a financial opportunity in selling.

Land, which unified families and communities historically, has been divisive for decades, Campbell explained. Conversations about who sold land and discussions about the amount they sold it for are constant. And often, the feeling is that people have sold below the land's true value. Word spreads, creating tension. Phoebe's husband, Henry (now deceased), told me that people would talk about the beachfront land they sold to the Marriott, saying he didn't get enough money for it. "They just cracking their mouth," he told me, meaning that it was meaningless gossip.

People in the community so often look at property as simply a source of material gain, according to Campbell, a way to make a quick buck, but they don't seem to see value in maintaining the land as part of their heritage. The divisiveness over land in recent decades has been compounded by the state's heirs' property laws. I spoke with Tish Lynn, a spokesperson for the Center for Heirs' Property Preservation, which seeks to prevent land loss, to offer more context about the problems Black families face with heirs' property. She said sometimes some heirs live on the land and pay taxes, and another heir with far less connection to the land sees an opportunity for financial gain. When the heir who isn't living on the land forces a sale, the entire family will lose property that has been in the family for generations. Even worse, predatory developers are sometimes able to identify land they're interested in developing on a tax map, then locate an heir who might live in another state and offer cash for ownership rights allowing the developer to force a sale, as if they're an heir. "It may be $1,000 that puts the whole property in jeopardy," said Lynn. "They [developers] are buying their rights to do what they have a right to do and force a sale."[21]

The Center for Heirs' Property offers legal resources to help families that want to hold on to their property to clear title to the land and create an agreement about how to maintain it, which often involves all heirs agreeing to share the tax burden. But rarely, she said, does the center get calls for assistance from Beaufort County, where Hilton Head is located. There's a particularly high level of distrust in discussing land issues in Beaufort.

"Hilton Head is the poster child for what we hope will not happen again," said Lynn. "It was an African American island lost into the hands of developers." Although Black people never owned most of Hilton Head, much of the most valuable land in the island's northern end that was Gullah-Geechee owned, like beachfront property, is gone.

A 2016 law, the Clementa C. Pinckney Uniform Heirs Property Act, offers some benefit to families who are interested in selling heirs' property because it requires magistrates who oversee sales of heirs' property to seek an amicable agreement among family members at the time of a sale. If one heir wants to sell, other heirs have the legal right to buy their interest to prevent the sale. While the law doesn't have a lot of teeth, it does require that heirs meet and attempt to negotiate an agreement.

Some leaders are trying to get people to understand that they can hold onto their land, said Campbell. And their families can benefit financially through long-term leasing to a developer that will generate income for generations. That's what the descendants of Benjamin White have done. White's descendants own acres of waterfront property off Squire Pope Road where Bluewater Resort & Marina is located. The timeshare company that owns the resort and marina is operating under a forty-year lease agreement. The family incorporated, said Campbell. They hold annual meetings, and all heirs derive monthly income from the property.

The Center for Heirs' Property Preservation has worked with a group of Black families from St. Helena that has owned 300 acres of waterfront land since the 1920s. The center was able to help clear title to a small piece of the land that was heirs' property so that land is no longer vulnerable to a forced sale. The family uses timber sales to cover their annual taxes and has a plan for maintaining the property well into the future. They hold annual family gatherings on the land. But such examples are rare, Lynn said. There are far more examples of people selling land to a developer who then flips the property and sells the land for twice the sales price a few days later.

Younger people don't seem to care about our own culture, Campbell said. "We have a lot of investment in cars and big houses we don't need." Even elderly people in their sixties or eighties have a gold rush mentality. They'll say: "I want to be rich before I die. "What's lacking, he said, is an understanding of the value of land in Gullah-Geechee heritage. "We don't have leadership in the family on cultural issues," he said. "One thing we have to do is teach our youngsters their beautiful history."

One positive sign in 2021 was the effort to maintain Gullah-Geechee land through the Gullah-Geechee Land and Cultural Preservation Task Force that was established by Hilton Head's Town Council. The Task Force works in part to help native islanders with resources to clear title to land. It is now working with the Hilton Head Heritage Library and University of South Carolina Beaufort to create an Heirs Property Family Research Project to help Gullah-Geechee families with heirs' property develop family trees that will provide the documentation needed to reach descendants and with the assistance of an attorney, they could secure title to the land and create a will that clarifies ownership.[22]

For Brown, the Gullah-Geechee community has gained a level of respect through the establishment of the Gullah-Geechee Cultural Heritage Corridor. And, he said, the 2017 creation of a chapter of the National Action Network, a national civil rights organization launched by Reverend Al Sharpton, helped the town's leadership to take the Gullah-Geechee community seriously. After the formation of the chapter, Gullah-Geechee activists called for a boycott of the RBC Heritage Golf Tournament, protesting ordinances that disadvantaged Gullah-Geechee residents such as burdensome rules that limit the ability to sell arts and crafts or food. "There was a threat to boycott the golf tournament and that got people's attention and that's how the Gullah-Geechee Task Force got commissioned and got a consultant to collaborate on all the plans that we developed," Brown said.

It's much easier for town officials to support something like Historic Mitchelville Freedom Park that can generate tourism income for Hilton Head, said Brown, than to grapple with the concerns that Gullah-Geechee have experienced and work on solutions. "It was easy for us and politicians to get behind something like Mitchelville. That's an economic driver. But when you start talking about the living and breathing people of the culture, that's a whole other story."

Conclusion

The research for this book grew out of a longing to know my family's story from a point of origin in West Africa through enslavement and emancipation. I wanted to know what my ancestors' lives were like and how they survived. While that quest is still ongoing and so many questions remain unanswered, in many ways it has been fulfilled.

Particularly important is learning that my family was part of one of the most African of Black cultures within the United States. And I have learned how the Gullah-Geechee of Hilton Head, like those on other islands in the region, chose a self-sustaining life of interdependence after enslavement, living apart from white people, creating community through their hard work and creativity.

The millions of African Americans who are descended from the Gullah-Geechee culture, like me, are ancestrally linked to a culture that maintained African spiritual concepts, music, rituals, foods, values, and a deep relationship to land, along with a Creole language that developed in West Africa. The Gullah-Geechee did not simply recreate the past but created new ways, drawing on the past to live in a new land under profoundly oppressive conditions. Their experience provides a window into one of the many ways African Americans have survived enslavement and systemic racial injustice, historically, across generations. Our ancestors, who were from culturally rich and sophisticated peoples, took agency to maintain what had meaning for them and created culture that was necessary to sustain themselves.

What the Gullah-Geechee forged drew from an amalgam of African ways of seeing and experiencing the world. The communal ways, bartering and giving, passing land down through extended families, and their sense of justice are a counterbalance to the individualism and materialism of American culture that create greater division. Our Gullah-Geechee ancestors show they were so much more than the physical labor their enslavers exploited.

Sancho and his mother Heena carried the memories of Africa forward in their names, like many thousands of Gullah-Geechee, leaving a gift for me and other descendants. Those names allow us to look into the past and remember who our ancestors were. With their effort to hold on to their heritage, remember Africa, and impart and recreate African-derived and inspired culture, it seems they intended to address the natal alienation our ancestors must have felt after being forcibly removed from their lands of origin. That longing to fill in the erasure of our pasts still resonates and reverberates for many African Americans today who like me, embark on journeys into our ancestral past.

Tracy Smith digs into her ancestral past in Alabama to "rescue stories" from the obscurity of the historical record of the powerful who dismiss the lives of the less powerful: "We are shedding light upon the flattening perspective of power, which tromps through the historical record, endowing some lives with innate value, and dismissing others outright."[1]

Rescuing whatever I could find of my ancestral stories, I have attempted to offer a small window to view the lives of Black Gullah-Geechee families who pushed for autonomy and so often sacrificed it out of economic need. So few pictures of the formerly enslaved exist on plantations in the South that the photo taken by Henry P. Moore in 1862 shows up again and again in articles, documentaries, and exhibitions about enslavement. With six ancestors among the formerly enslaved on Fish Haul, almost definitely including my ancestors, the photo adds something of their lives, their dignity, their purposefulness, and the African culture displayed in their dress.

Sancho and his brothers-in-law, Adam and Jacob, had the distinction of being among the 185,000 African Americans who helped end slavery. And they were fortunate enough to see the Civil War end in the port city where the war began—a city through which nearly 50 percent of enslaved Africans were brought to these shores. Adam was among the residents of Mitchelville, the all-Black self-governing town created by the federal government during the Civil War. But more important, they had one of the rare opportunities African Americans have had in this nation: to create a Black space, largely free from Jim Crow and its structures. Despite difficult lives, enslaved until adulthood and with ailments and deteriorating bodies in their early sixties, they thrived in many ways.

Hilton Head's Gullah-Geechee families associated land ownership with liberation where they had been enslaved, forming communities and doing everything for themselves, building homes and boats, fishing and farming, educating their young, delivering future generations and healing themselves from illness. The Gullah-Geechee inspire hope through their demonstration of what people stuck on the very bottom rung of American society as enslaved Black people on cotton plantations in the Deep South were capable of when freed. But while this Black space offered psychological benefits, it came at a price.

The material poverty, the lack of infrastructure and institutions of higher education, and the paucity of economic opportunities shaped by the invisible hands of Jim Crow led so many Gullah-Geechee, including my relatives, to flee Hilton Head for cities in the industrialized North. The socioeconomic progress many achieved was impossible without leaving. Aggressive gentrification in recent decades has also marginalized Hilton Head's Gullah-Geechee. Yet thousands still live there and own land their ancestors bought after the Civil War.

This journey has manifested the value of looking into the past to find out some of what wasn't shared. Older generations in my family (like my Aunt Aggie, who grew up around formerly enslaved men and women) may have felt a need to distance themselves from the trauma of enslavement. For current generations, knowing that past where it happened, how our ancestors persevered during and after enslavement is essential. If we know only of a grandparent's birthplace in the South and little else, it leaves us with a greater void and knowledge erased.

While there's much I don't know, I can now see my ancestors, including parents' and grandparents' lives dating back some 175 years. With recent DNA analysis, 5th-8th cousins who are descended from Igbo and Yoruba peoples show up. I don't know the names, stories, or birthplaces of those Igbo and Yoruba ancestors who were first enslaved. But in Hilton Head where my ancestors' bones lay I feel a very deep spiritual connection. I'm inspired and humbled to be a part of the Gullah-Geechee family, a northern cousin, and grateful to have had this opportunity to tell stories about Hilton Head's heritage. The pain our ancestors and relatives endured is an indelible part of their past, but so, too, is the beauty, resilience and strength of their culture.

Notes

Preface

1. Morgan Jerkins, *Wandering in Strange Lands: A Daughter of the Great Migration Reclaims Her Roots* (New York: Harper, 2020), 5–6.
2. Jerkins, *Wandering in Strange Lands*, 6.
3. Goff, Jon-Sesrie, dir. *After Sherman.* Hedera Pictures, 2022.
4. Jerkins, *Wandering in Strange Lands*, 237.
5. Dash, Julie, dir. *Daughters of the Dust.* Kino International, 1991.
6. Goff, *After Sherman.*
7. Tracy K. Smith, *To Free the Captives: A Plea for the American Soul* (New York: Knopf, 2023), 10.
8. Wilbur Cross and Eric Crawford, *Gullah Culture in America*, 2nd ed. (Durham, NC: Blair, 2023), 13.
9. National Park Service, *Low Country Gullah Culture Special Resource Study and Final Environmental Impact Statement* (Atlanta, GA: National Park Service, Southeast Regional Office, July 2005), 54.
10. Douglas R. Egerton, *Thunder at the Gates: The Black Civil War Regiments That Redeemed America* (New York: Basic Books, 2016), 336.

Introduction

1. Edda L. Fields-Black, COMBEE: Harriet Tubman, the Combahee River Raid, and Black Freedom during the Civil War (New York: Oxford University Press, 2024), xxiv.
2. Christopher Sancho, Military Service Record. U.S.C.T. 21. D167.P.97.73–2200. 83–195.129. National Archives, Washington, DC.
3. Joseph A. Opala, *The Gullah: Rice, Slavery, and the Sierra Leone-American Connection* (Washington, DC: United States Information Service, 1987), 1.
4. National Park Service, *Low Country Gullah Culture*, 13.
5. Emory Campbell, interview with author, August 16, 2018.
6. Opala, *The Gullah*, 9.
7. National Park Service, *Low Country Gullah Culture*, 5, D9.
8. National Park Service, *Low Country Gullah Culture*, 13.
9. Thomas C. Barnwell Jr., Emory Shaw Campbell, and Carolyn Grant, *Gullah Days: Hilton Head Islanders Before the Bridge 1861–1956* (Durham, NC: Blair, 2020), 78.
10. Barnwell et al., *Gullah Days*, 78.
11. National Park Service, *Low Country Gullah Culture*, 10.
12. National Park Service, *Low Country Gullah Culture*, 54.

Chapter 1: The Rice Connection

1. Michael W. Twitty, The Cooking Gene: A Journey Through African American Culinary History in the Old South (New York: Amistad, 2017), 259–60.
2. Judith A. Carney, *Black Rice: The African Origins of Rice Cultivation in the Americas* (Cambridge, MA: Harvard University Press, 2002), 90.
3. Carney, *Black Rice*, 39.
4. Twitty, *The Cooking Gene*, 244.
5. Carney, *Black Rice*, 80.
6. Carney, *Black Rice*, 62.
7. Carney, *Black Rice*, 13.
8. Carney, *Black Rice*, 5.
9. Kim Severson, "Finding a Lost Strain of Rice and Clues to Slave Cooking," *New York Times*, February 13, 2018.
10. Carney, *Black Rice*, 85–86.
11. Carney, *Black Rice*, 89.
12. Twitty, *The Cooking Gene*, 250.
13. Carney, *Black Rice*, 129–31.
14. Twitty, *The Cooking Gene*, 245–46.
15. Cross and Crawford, *Gullah Culture in America*, 202.
16. Twitty, *The Cooking Gene*, 247.
17. B. J. Dennis, interview with author, June 29, 2018.
18. Twitty, *The Cooking Gene*, 261.

Chapter 2: A State Rooted in Slavery

1. Ethan J. Kytle and Blain Roberts, Denmark Vesey's Garden: Slavery and Memory in the Cradle of the Confederacy (New York: The New Press, 2018), 12.
2. Chester B. Depratter, "The Yamasee War: 1715–1717." South Carolina Archaeology Month 2015, University of South Carolina, South Carolina Institute of Archaeology and Anthropology. Columbia, October 2015.
3. Mary Battle and Christopher Sawula, "African Passages, Lowcountry Adaptations," College of Charleston, 2013. Online exhibition. https://ldhi .library.cofc.edu/exhibits/show/africanpassageslowcountryadapt
4. Battle and Sawula, "African Passages."
5. Depratter, "The Yamasee War."
6. Depratter, "The Yamasee War."
7. Depratter, "The Yamasee War."
8. Depratter, "The Yamasee War."
9. Elizabeth Brabec and Sharon Richardson, "A Clash of Cultures: The Landscape of the Sea Island Gullah," *Landscape Journal* 26, no. 1 (January 2007): 153.

10. Brabec and Richardson, "A Clash of Cultures," 153.
11. Dana E. Byrd, with Tyler DeAngelis, "Tracing Transformations: Hilton Head Island's Journey to Freedom, 1860–1865," *Nineteenth-Century Art Worldwide* 14, no. 3 (2015): 10.
12. Brabec and Richardson, "A Clash of Cultures," 153.
13. Kytle and Roberts, *Denmark Vesey's Garden*, 15.
14. Kytle and Roberts, *Denmark Vesey's Garden*, 15.
15. Byrd with DeAngelis, "Tracing Transformations."
16. Byrd with DeAngelis, "Tracing Transformations."
17. Barnwell et al., *Gullah Days*, 154.
18. Brabec and Richardson, "A Clash of Cultures," 153.

Chapter 3: What's in a Name?
1. Lorenzo Dow Turner, *Africanisms in the Gullah Dialect*, introduction by Katherine Wyly Mille and Michael B. Montgomery (Columbia: University of South Carolina Press, 2002).
2. David E. Skinner, "Mande Settlement and the Development of Islamic Institutions in Sierra Leone," *The International Journal of African Historical Studies* 11, no. 1 (1978): 45.
3. Skinner, "Mande Settlement," 37, 50.
4. Basil Davidson, *Africa in History*, rev. ed. (New York: Touchstone Books, 1995), 98; Joseph Opala, interview with author, July 1, 2018.
5. Davidson, *Africa in History*, 90.
6. Skinner, "Mande Settlement," 32.
7. Opala, interview with author, May 22, 2021.
8. Walter Rodney, *A History of the Upper Guinea Coast, 1545–1800* (New York: Monthly Review Press, 1970).
9. James Thayer, interview with author, June 29, 2021.
10. Philip D. Morgan, *Slave Counterpoint: Black Culture in the Eighteenth-Century Chesapeake and Lowcountry* (Chapel Hill: Omohundro Institute and University of North Carolina Press, 1998), 454.
11. Turner, *Africanisms in the Gullah Dialect*, 93.
12. National Park Service, *Low Country Gullah Culture*, D8.
13. Turner, *Africanisms in the Gullah Dialect*, 128.
14. Charles Joyner, *Down by the Riverside: A South Carolina Slave Community*, 25th anniversary edition (Urbana: University of Illinois Press, 2009), 218.
15. Joyner, *Down by the Riverside*, 219.
16. Turner, *Africanisms in the Gullah Dialect*, 64.
17. Turner, *Africanisms in the Gullah Dialect*, 112.
18. Turner, *Africanisms in the Gullah Dialect*, 156.
19. Rodney, *A History of the Upper Guinea Coast*, 6.

20. Rodney, *A History of the Upper Guinea Coast*, 24, 32.
21. Rodney, *A History of the Upper Guinea Coast*, 117.
22. Rodney, *A History of the Upper Guinea Coast*, 256.
23. Rodney, *A History of the Upper Guinea Coast*, 256.
24. Michelle D. Commander, *Afro-Atlantic Flight: Speculative Returns and the Black Fantastic*, illustrated edition (Durham, NC: Duke University Press, 2017).

Chapter 4: The Battle for Emancipation
1. Byrd with DeAngelis, "Tracing Transformations."
2. Kevin Dougherty, *The Port Royal Experiment: A Case Study in Development*, illustrated edition (Jackson: University Press of Mississippi, 2014), 7.
3. Dougherty, *The Port Royal Experiment*, 9, 10, 12.
4. Dougherty, *The Port Royal Experiment*, 14–15.
5. Byrd with DeAngelis, "Tracing Transformations."
6. Michael Shapiro, "Rehearsal for Reconstruction," *New York Times*, November 6, 2011.
7. Slave Narratives. A Folk History of Slavery in the United States. Interviews with Former Slaves. Federal Writers' Project. 1936–38. Library of Congress, Washington, DC. https://www.loc.gov/item/mesn143/.
8. Dougherty, *The Port Royal Experiment*, 19.
9. Akiko Ochiai, "The Port Royal Experiment Revisited: Northern Visions of Reconstruction and the Land Question," *The New England Quarterly* 74, no. 1 (2001): 94–95.
10. Dougherty, *The Port Royal Experiment*, 21.
11. Dougherty, *The Port Royal Experiment*, 21.
12. Dougherty, *The Port Royal Experiment*, 23–25.
13. Dougherty, *The Port Royal Experiment*, 26.
14. Byrd with DeAngelis, "Tracing Transformations."
15. Dougherty, *The Port Royal Experiment*, 28.
16. Dougherty, *The Port Royal Experiment*, 55.
17. Dougherty, *The Port Royal Experiment*, 29–30.
18. Dougherty, *The Port Royal Experiment*, 25.
19. Dougherty, *The Port Royal Experiment*, 55–57.
20. Dougherty, *The Port Royal Experiment*, 34.
21. Dougherty, *The Port Royal Experiment*, 90–92.
22. Michael Trinkley, ed., *An Archaeological Survey of the Barker Field Expansion Project, Hilton Head Island, Beaufort County, South Carolina*, Research Series 17 (Columbia, SC: Chicora Foundation, August 1989), 19.
23. Dougherty, *The Port Royal Experiment*, 99.

24. Trinkley, *An Archaeological Survey of the Barker Field*, 23.
25. Ahmad Ward, interview with author, February 16, 2018.
26. J. M. W., "A Negro Conventicle—The Rev. Abraham Murchison—Trip to Seabrook—The Drayton Plantation—The Elliott Plantation—Rose and Her Family—A Negro Bayoneted—The Contrabands at Seabrook—A Human Phenomenon—Cotton Planting—The Bombardment of Fort Pulaski to Commence," *New York Times*, April 19, 1862.
27. Nancy Burke, Patricia A. Burke, and Susie Marquis, *They Served: Stories of United States Colored Troops from Hilton Head, South Carolina*, edited by Nancy M. Burke (Hilton Head, SC: Heritage Library Foundation, 2017), 1–2.
28. Burke et al., *They Served*, 1–2.
29. Kate Clifford Larson, Bound for the Promised Land: Harriet Tubman: Portrait of an American Hero (New York: One World, 2004), 212.
30. Fields-Black, *COMBEE*, 166.
31. Burke et al., *They Served*, 5.
32. Burke et al., *They Served*, 5.
33. Burke et al., *They Served*, 5.
34. Disability Pension file of Samuel Christopher alias Sanco Christopher, Bureau of Pensions. Soldier's Certificate No. 933856, Widow's Certificate No. 786563. National Archives, Washington, DC.
35. Blain Roberts and Ethan J. Kytle, "When Freedom Came to Charleston," *New York Times*, February 19, 2015, https://archive.nytimes.com/opinionator.blogs.nytimes.com/2015/02/19/.
36. Roberts and Kytle, "When Freedom Came."
37. David Blight, "Forgetting Why We Remember," *New York Times*, May 29, 2011.
38. Sewell Chan, "The Unofficial History of Memorial Day," *New York Times*, May 26, 2018.
39. Barnwell et al., *Gullah Days*, 168.
40. Barton, Tom, "Making Mitchelville Real: Dig Unearths Hilton Head's Freedmen's Past, *The Island Packet*, August 26, 2014.
41. Barnwell et al., *Gullah Days*, 57.
42. Ahmad Ward, interview with author, February 16, 2018.
43. Larson, Bound for the Promised Land, 216.
44. Letter from Clara Barton to "Aimee," Clara Barton National Historic Site, CLBA4490. National Park Service, Washington, DC. https://www.nps.gov/museum/exhibits/clba/exb/work/civil_war/clba4490_letterfront.html.
45. Dougherty, *The Port Royal Experiment*, 9.
46. Ward, interview with author.

Chapter 5: The Land that Liberates

1. Dougherty, The Port Royal Experiment, 109.
2. "Newspaper Account of a Meeting between Black Religious Leaders and Union Military Authorities," February 13, 1865, Freedom and Southern Society Project. University of Maryland. https://freedmen.umd.edu /savmtg.htm.
3. Rick Beard, "Forty Acres and a Mule," *New York Times*, January 16, 2015.
4. "Newspaper Account of a Meeting."
5. Beard, "Forty Acres and a Mule."
6. William A. Gladstone, William A. Gladstone Afro-American Military Collection: Special Field Orders, No. 15, Headquarters, Military Division of the Mississippi, by Major General W. T. Sherman, re "young and able-bodied negroes must be encouraged to enlist," mentions bounties paid and locations for settlement of freed Negro, 1865. Manuscript/mixed Material. https://www.loc.gov/item/mss83434256/.
7. Henry Louis Gates Jr., "The Truth Behind 40 Acres and a Mule," PBS, https://www.pbs.org/wnet/african-americans-many-rivers-to-cross /history/the-truth-behind-40-acres-and-a-mule/.
8. W. E. B. Du Bois, *Black Reconstruction in America*, edited by Henry Louis Gates Jr. (New York: Oxford University Press, 2007), 185.
9. Du Bois, *Black Reconstruction in America*, 495–96.
10. US, Freedman's Bank Records, 1865–1874, Ancestry.com, https://www .ancestry.com/search/collections/8755/.
11. Ochiai, "The Port Royal Experiment Revisited," 98.
12. Ochiai, "The Port Royal Experiment Revisited," 99.
13. Ochiai, "The Port Royal Experiment Revisited," 100.
14. Ochiai, "The Port Royal Experiment Revisited," 100–101.
15. Brabec and Richardson, "A Clash of Cultures," 160.
16. Head of Family Land Certificate. Heritage Library History & Ancestry Research Center. Jenkins, Adam, Certificate Nos. #0925, #1171.
17. Brabec and Richardson, "A Clash of Cultures," 157.
18. Trinkley, *An Archaeological Survey of the Barker Field*, 100–101.
19. Scott Butler et al., "Archaeological Data Recovery at Mitchelville Hilton Head Island Airport Improvements Study Area," Beaufort County Improvement Study, December 2013, 28.
20. Butler et al., "Archaeological Data Recovery at Mitchelville" 28.
21. Butler et al., "Archaeological Data Recovery at Mitchelville," 228.
22. Michael Trinkley, *Indian and Freedmen Occupation at the Fish Haul Site* Research Series 7 (Columbia, SC: Chicora Foundation, 2020), 102.
23. Butler et al., "Archaeological Data Recovery at Mitchelville," 30.
24. Burke et al., *They Served*, 41, 71, 105.

25. Michael N. Danielson, *Profits and Politics in Paradise: The Development of Hilton Head Island* (Columbia: University of South Carolina Press, 1995), 10.

26. Barnwell et al., *Gullah Days*, 82.

27. Byrd with DeAngelis, "Tracing Transformations."

28. Butler, et al., "Archaeological Data Recovery at Mitchelville," 30.

29. "Index to Hilton Head Deeds 1863–1899," Heritage Library Ancestry and Research Center. https://static1.squarespace.com/static/5802c4d 9414fb5e45ce4dc44/t/5dfa8bd6de0331433df831e7/1576700889993 /Property+Transactions.pdf.

30. Butler et al., "Archaeological Data Recovery at Mitchelville," 30.

31. Danielson, *Profits and Politics in Paradise*,12.

Chapter 6: The Ancestors Find Their Way

1. Deposition of Samuel Christopher alias Sanco Christopher, Bureau of Pensions, US National Archives. October 29, 1901.

2. Butler et al., "Archaeological Data Recovery at Mitchelville," 9.

3. Deposition of Samuel Christopher.

4. Barnwell et al., *Gullah Days*, 252.

5. US, Freedman's Bank Records, 1865–1874.

6. 1868 SC Voter Registration Bluffton and Hilton Head Electoral District. Heritage Library History & Ancestry Research Center.

7. 1868 Federal Agricultural Census Hilton Head Island, compiled by Dorothy Arwe. Heritage Library History & Ancestry Research Center.

8. Disability Pension file of Samuel Christopher.

9. Dorothy R. Arwe, transcriber,."1870 Federal Census St. Luke's Parish," Beaufort County, Heritage Library History & Ancestry Research Center.

10. Burke et al., *They Served*, 46.

11. W. Calvin Smith, "Habersham Family," New Georgia Encyclopedia, last modified Sept. 11, 2014, https://www.georgiaencyclopedia.org/articles /history-archaeology/habersham-family/.

12. Pension File. Certificate No. 933856.

13. Burke et al., *They Served*, 47.

14. Pension File. Certificate No. 933856.

15. Disability Pension file of Moses Polite, Bureau of Pensions. Soldier's Certificate No. 969978. National Archives, Washington, DC.

16. Jennifer Schuessler, "Smallpox Took a Huge Toll on Emancipated Slaves, Historian Writes," *Seattle Times*, June 16, 2012.

17. Burke et al., *They Served*, 46.

18. Disability Pension file of Samuel Christopher.

19. Disability Pension file of Samuel Christopher.

20. Disability Pension file of Samuel Christopher.
21. Disability Pension file of Adam Jenkins. Bureau of Pensions, Soldier's Certificate No. 720739. National Archives, Washington, DC.
22. Disability Pension file of Adam Jenkins.
23. Orlando Patterson, *Slavery and Social Death: A Comparative Study, with a New Preface*. 2nd ed. (Cambridge, MA: Harvard University Press, 2018), 5.
24. Disability Pension file of Adam Jenkins.
25. Disability Pension file of Adam Jenkins.
26. Head of Family Land Certificate, Nos. #0925, #1171.
27. Disability Pension file of Adam Jenkins.
28. Disability Pension file of Adam Jenkins.
29. Butler et al., "Archaeological Data Recovery at Mitchelville," 197.
30. Burke et al., *They Served*, 105.
31. Burke et al., *They Served*, 105.
32. Fields-Black, *COMBEE*, xxiv.
33. Butler et al., "Archaeological Data Recovery at Mitchelville," 34.
34. Disability Pension file of Jacob Jenkins, Bureau of Pensions. Soldier's Certificate Nos. 526865, 1060194. National Archives, Washington, DC.
35. Burke et al., *They Served*, 107.
36. Disability Pension file of Jacob Jenkins.
37. Burke et al., *They Served*, 107.
38. Disability Pension file of Jacob Jenkins.
39. Burke et al., *They Served*, 107–8.
40. Burke et al., *They Served*, 107.
41. 1868 Federal Agricultural Census.
42. Burke et al., *They Served*, 107.
43. Disability Pension file of Jacob Jenkins.
44. Burke et al., *They Served*, 107–8.

Chapter 7: Speaking Gullah

1. Opala, *The Gullah*, 7.
2. Opala, *The Gullah*, 7.
3. Opala, *The Gullah*, 7.
4. Opala, *The Gullah*, 8.
5. National Park Service, *Low Country Gullah Culture*, D20.
6. National Park Service, *Low Country Gullah Culture*, D27.
7. Joyner, *Down by the Riverside*, 220.
8. Joyner, *Down by the Riverside*, 220.
9. National Park Service, *Low Country Gullah Culture*, F17.
10. National Park Service, *Low Country Gullah Culture*, D27.

11. Mille, Katherine Wyly and Michael B. Montgomery. Introduction to *Africanisms in the Gullah Dialect*, by Lorenzo Dow Turner, xxiv. (Columbia: University of South Carolina Press, 2002).

12. Jessica R. Berry, interview with author, April 6, 2018.

13. Jessica R. Berry, "A Native Scholar's Perspective on the Gullah/Geechee Language Barrier," *Post and Courier*, December 24, 2016.

14. Campbell, interview with author.

15. Mille and Montgomery, *Africanisms*, xxxii.

16. Emory Campbell, Gullah Cultural Legacies: A Synopsis of Gullah Traditions, Customary Beliefs, Art Forms and Speech on Hilton Head Island and Vicinal Sea Islands in South Carolina and Georgia (North Charleston, SC: BookSurge, 2008), 57–58.

Chapter 8: Life before and after the Bridge

1. Carrier, Tim, dir. *Family Across the Sea*. South Carolina Educational Network, 1990.

2. Campbell, interview with author.

3. Campbell, "Gullah Geechee Culture: Respected, Understood and Striving: Sixty Years after Lorenzo Dow Turner's Masterpiece, *Africanisms in the Gullah Dialect*," *The Black Scholar* 41, no. 1 (2011): 81–83.

4. Barnwell et al., *Gullah Days*, 253–54.

5. Faith Mitchell, *Hoodoo Medicine: Gullah Herbal Remedies*, Rev. ed. (Columbia, SC: Summerhouse Press, 1999), 31.

6. Mitchell, *Hoodoo Medicine*, 32–33.

7. Mitchell, *Hoodoo Medicine*, 34.

8. Cross and Crawford, *Gullah Culture in America*, 130.

9. Barnwell et al., *Gullah Days*, 245.

10. Danielson, *Profits and Politics in Paradise*.

11. Danielson, *Profits and Politics in Paradise*, 11.

12. Danielson, *Profits and Politics in Paradise*, 12.

13. Carol Motsinger and Daniel J. Gross, "His Ancestors Fought for Their Freedom in the Civil War. Now, He Fights to Preserve What They Left Him," *Greenville News*, July 20, 2021.

14. Danielson, *Profits and Politics in Paradise*, 13–14.

15. Butler et al., "Archaeological Data Recovery at Mitchelville," 30.

16. Danielson, *Profits and Politics in Paradise*, 14.

17. Danielson, *Profits and Politics in Paradise*, 14–15.

18. Danielson, *Profits and Politics in Paradise*, 16.

19. Danielson, *Profits and Politics in Paradise*, 39.

20. Danielson, *Profits and Politics in Paradise*, 41.

21. Danielson, *Profits and Politics in Paradise*, 41.

22. Danielson, *Profits and Politics in Paradise*, 43.
23. Danielson, *Profits and Politics in Paradise*, 83–85.
24. Danielson, *Profits and Politics in Paradise*, 51.
25. Danielson, *Profits and Politics in Paradise*, 18.
26. Katherine Kokal, "Business Once Boomed in These Hilton Head Gullah Neighborhoods. Why They're Empty Now," *Island Packet*, August 24, 2020.
27. Katherine Kokal, "Black Families in Hilton Head's Gated 'Plantations' Call for Changes Close to Home," *Island Packet*, June 21, 2020.

Chapter 9: A Gullah-Geechee Family's Ties

1. Phoebe Driessen, interview with author, August 15, 2021.
2. Campbell, *Gullah Cultural Legacies*, 102.
3. Barnwell et al., *Gullah Days*, 319.
4. Ryan Copeland, "How Beaufort's Mather School Changed Lives in the Past—and Can Inform Our Present" *Island Packet*, September 6, 2017.
5. Mary Bryant, interview with author, February 19, 2018. Mary passed away six months after the interview.
6. Disability Pension file of Adam Jenkins.
7. Barnwell et al., *Gullah Days*, 301.

Chapter 10: Where Religion and Justice Intersect

1. National Park Service, *Low Country Gullah Culture*, 75.
2. LeRhonda S. Manigault-Bryant, *Talking to the Dead: Religion, Music, and Lived Memory among Gullah/Geechee Women* (Durham, NC: Duke University Press, 2014), 37–38.
3. Burke et al., *They Served*, 101.
4. National Park Service, *Low Country Gullah Culture*, 69.
5. National Park Service, *Low Country Gullah Culture*, 86.
6. National Park Service, *Low Country Gullah Culture*, 69.
7. Barnwell et al., *Gullah Days*, 261, 263.
8. Manigault-Bryant, *Talking to the Dead*, 120–22.
9. Manigault-Bryant, *Talking to the Dead*, 133.
10. National Park Service, "Low Country Gullah Culture," D31.
11. Elijah Heyward III, interview with author, October 18, 2023.
12. National Park Service, *Low Country Gullah Culture*, F14.
13. Barnwell et al., *Gullah Days*, 277–78.
14. Michael A. Gomez, Exchanging Our Country Marks: The Transformation of African Identities in the Colonial and Antebellum South (Chapel Hill: University of North Carolina Press, 1998), 100.
15. Gomez, Exchanging Our Country Marks, 99.

Chapter 12: The Double-Edged Sword

1. Bamidele A. Demerson, "Family Life on Wadmalaw Island," in *Sea Island Roots: African Presence in the Carolinas and Georgia*, edited by Keith E. Baird and Mary A. Twining (Trenton, NJ: Africa World Press, 1991), 57, 65.
2. Demerson, "Family Life on Wadmalaw Island," 65.
3. Christopher, interview with author.
4. Demerson, "Family Life on Wadmalaw Island," 59.
5. Demerson, "Family Life on Wadmalaw Island," 66.
6. Demerson, "Family Life on Wadmalaw Island," 61.
7. Demerson, "Family Life on Wadmalaw Island," 70.
8. Gomez, *Exchanging Our Country Marks*, 128.
9. Driessen, interview with author.
10. Equal Justice Initiative. "Lynching in America," 14–15.25.
11. Equal Justice Initiative. "Lynching in America," 17
12. Barnwell et al., *Gullah Days*, 97.
13. Barnwell et al., *Gullah Days*, 107.
14. Barnwell et al., *Gullah Days*, 232–35.
15. Barnwell et al., *Gullah Days*, 237.
16. Motsinger and Gross, "His Ancestors Fought."
17. Alex Brown, interview with author, September 20, 2020.
18. Blake Douglass, "Hilton Head, Beaufort County Officials Clash on St. James Baptist Church relocation," *Island Packet*, May 12, 2023.
19. Motsinger and Gross, "His Ancestors Fought."
20. Motsinger and Gross, "His Ancestors Fought."
21. Tish Lynn, interview with author, July 6, 2018.
22. Associated Press, "New Research Could Help Preserve Gullah-Geechee Lands," South Carolina Public Radio, August 15, 2021.

Conclusion

1. Smith, *To Free the Captives*, 25.

Bibliography

1868 SC Voter Registration Bluffton and Hilton Head Electoral District. Heritage Library History & Ancestry Research Center.

Arwe, Dorothy R., transcriber. "1868 Federal Agricultural Census Hilton Head Island." Beaufort County, Heritage Library History & Ancestry Research Center.

Arwe, Dorothy R. "1870 Federal Census St. Luke's Parish." Beaufort County, Heritage Library History & Ancestry Research Center.

Associated Press. "New Research Could Help Preserve Gullah-Geechee Lands." South Carolina Public Radio, August 15, 2021.

Barnwell, Thomas C., Jr., Emory Shaw Campbell, and Carolyn Grant. *Gullah Days: Hilton Head Islanders Before the Bridge 1861–1956*. Illustrated edition. Durham, NC: Blair, 2020.

Barton, Tom, "Making Mitchelville Real: Dig Unearths Hilton Head's Freedmen's Past, *The Island Packet*, August 24, 2014.

Battle, Mary, and Christopher Sawula. "African Passages, Lowcountry Adaptations." College of Charleston, 2013. Online exhibition. https://ldhi.library .cofc.edu/exhibits/show/africanpassageslowcountryadapt.

Beard, Rick. "Forty Acres and a Mule." *New York Times*, January 16, 2015.

Berry, Jessica R. "A Native Scholar's Perspective on the Gullah/Geechee Language Barrier." *Post and Courier*, December 24, 2016.

Blight, David. "Forgetting Why We Remember." *New York Times*, May 29, 2011.

Brabec, Elizabeth, and Sharon Richardson. "A Clash of Cultures: The Landscape of the Sea Island Gullah." *Landscape Journal* 26, no. 1 (January 2007): 151–67.

Burke, Nancy, Patricia A. Burke, and Susie Marquis. *They Served: Stories of United States Colored Troops from Hilton Head, South Carolina*. Edited by Nancy M. Burke. Hilton Head, NC: Heritage Library Foundation, 2017.

Brady, Meagan, Scott Butler, Jeff Sherard, and Patricia Stallings. "Archaeological Data Recovery at Mitchelville Hilton Head Island Airport Improvements Study Area." Beaufort County Improvement Study, December 2013.

Byrd, Dana E., with Tyler DeAngelis. "Tracing Transformations: Hilton Head Island's Journey to Freedom, 1860–1865." *Nineteenth-Century Art Worldwide* 14, no. 3 (2015). https://19thc-artworldwide.org/autumn15/byrd -tracing-transformations-introduction.

Campbell, Emory. *Gullah Cultural Legacies: A Synopsis of Gullah Traditions, Customary Beliefs, Art Forms and Speech on Hilton Head Island and Vicinal Sea Islands in South Carolina and Georgia*. North Charleston, SC: BookSurge, 2008.

Campbell, Emory. "Gullah Geechee Culture: Respected, Understood and Striving: Sixty Years after Lorenzo Dow Turner's Masterpiece, *Africanisms in the Gullah Dialect*." *The Black Scholar* 41, no. 1 (2011): 77–84. https://doi.org/10.5816/blackscholar.41.1.0077.

Carney, Judith A. *Black Rice: The African Origins of Rice Cultivation in the Americas*. Cambridge, MA: Harvard University Press, 2002.

Carrier, Tim, dir. *Family Across the Sea*. South Carolina Educational Network, 1990

Chan, Sewell. "The Unofficial History of Memorial Day." *New York Times*, May 26, 2018.

Christopher Sancho. Military Service Record. U.S.C.T. 21. D167.P.97.73–2200. 83–195.129. National Archives, Washington, DC.

Commander, Michelle D. *Afro-Atlantic Flight: Speculative Returns and the Black Fantastic*. Illustrated edition. Durham, NC: Duke University Press, 2017.

Copeland, Ryan. "How Beaufort's Mather School Changed Lives in the Past— and Can Inform Our Present" *Island Packet*, September 6, 2017.

Cross, Wilbur, and Eric Crawford. *Gullah Culture in America*. 2nd ed. Durham, NC: Blair, 2023.

Danielson, Michael N. *Profits and Politics in Paradise: The Development of Hilton Head Island*. Columbia: University of South Carolina Press, 1995.

Dash, Julie, dir. *Daughters of the Dust*. Kino International, 1991.

Davidson, Basil. *Africa in History*. Rev. ed. New York: Touchstone Books, 1995.

Demerson, Bamidele A. "Family Life on Wadmalaw Island." In *Sea Island Roots: African Presence in the Carolinas and Georgia*, edited by Keith E. Baird and Mary A. Twining, 57–87. Trenton, NJ: Africa World Press, 1991.

Deposition of Samuel Christopher alias Sanco Christopher. Bureau of Pensions. US National Archives. October 29, 1901.

DePratter, Chester B. South Carolina Institute of Archaeology and Anthropology—University of South Carolina. Archaeology Month Poster— The Yamasee War: 1715–1717, 2015. Columbia: University of South Carolina, South Carolina Institute of Archaeology and Anthropology, 2015.

Disability Pension file of Adam Jenkins. Bureau of Pensions. Soldier's Certificate No. 720739. National Archives, Washington, DC.

Disability Pension file of Jacob Jenkins. Bureau of Pensions. Soldier's Certificate Nos. 526865, 1060194. National Archives, Washington, DC.

Disability Pension file of Moses Polite. Bureau of Pensions. Soldier's Certificate No. 969978. National Archives, Washington, DC.

Disability Pension file of Samuel Christopher alias Sanco Christopher. Bureau of Pensions. Soldier's Certificate No. 933856, Widow's Certificate No. 786563. National Archives, Washington, DC.

Dougherty, Kevin. *The Port Royal Experiment: A Case Study in Development*. Illustrated edition. Jackson: University Press of Mississippi, 2014.

Douglass, Blake. "Hilton Head, Beaufort County Officials Clash on St. James Baptist Church Relocation." *Island Packet*, May 12, 2023.

Du Bois, W. E. B. *Black Reconstruction in America*, edited by Henry Louis Gates Jr. New York: Oxford University Press, 2007.

Egerton, Douglas R. *Thunder at the Gates: The Black Civil War Regiments That Redeemed America*. Illustrated edition. New York: Basic Books, 2016.

Equal Justice Initiative. "Lynching in America: Confronting the Legacy of Racial Terror." 2017. https://eji.org/wp-content/uploads/2005/11/lynching -in-america-3d-ed-052421.pdf.

Fields-Black, Edda L. *COMBEE: Harriet Tubman, the Combahee River Raid, and Black Freedom during the Civil War*. New York: Oxford University Press, 2024.

Gates, Henry Louis, Jr. "The Truth Behind 40 Acres and a Mule." PBS. https:// www.pbs.org/wnet/african-americans-many-rivers-to-cross/history/the -truth-behind-40-acres-and-a-mule/.

Gladstone, William A. William A. Gladstone Afro-American Military Collection: Special Field Orders, No. 15, Headquarters, Military Division of the Mississippi, by Major General W. T. Sherman, re "young and able-bodied negroes must be encouraged to enlist," mentions bounties paid and locations for settlement of freed Negro. 1865. Library of Congress, Manuscript/ mixed material. https://www.loc.gov/item/mss83434256/.

Goff, Jon-Sesrie, dir. *After Sherman*. Hedera Pictures, 2022.

Gomez, Michael A. *Exchanging Our Country Marks: The Transformation of African Identities in the Colonial and Antebellum South*. Chapel Hill: University of North Carolina Press, 1998.

Head of Family Land Certificate. Heritage Library History & Ancestry Research Center. Jenkins, Adam, Certificate Nos. #0925, #1171.

"Index to Hilton Head Deeds 1863–1899." Heritage Library Ancestry and Research Center. https://static1.squarespace.com/static/5802c4d9414fb 5e45ce4dc44/t/5dfa8bd6de0331433df831e7/1576700889993/Property +Transactions.pdf.

"Index to Land Certificates Sold to Heads of Families of the African Race, 1863–1872." Heritage Library Ancestry and Research Center. https:// heritagelib.org/land-certificates-a

J.M.W. "Negro Conventicle—The Rev. Abraham Murchison—Trip to Seabrook—The Drayton Plantation—The Elliott Plantation—Rose and Her Family—A Negro Bayoneted—The Contrabands at Seabrook—A Human Phenomenon—Cotton Planting—The Bombardment of Fort Pulaski to Commence." *New York Times*, April 19, 1862.

Jerkins, Morgan. *Wandering in Strange Lands: A Daughter of the Great Migration Reclaims Her Roots*. Illustrated edition. New York: Harper, 2020.

Joyner, Charles. *Down by the Riverside: A South Carolina Slave Community*. 25th Anniversary Edition. Urbana: University of Illinois Press, 2009.

Kokal, Katherine. "Black Families in Hilton Head's Gated 'Plantations' Call for Changes Close to Home." *Island Packet*, June 21, 2020.

Kokal, Katherine. "Business Once Boomed in These Hilton Head Gullah Neighborhoods. Why They're Empty Now." *Island Packet*, August 24, 2020.

Kytle, Ethan J., and Blain Roberts. *Denmark Vesey's Garden: Slavery and Memory in the Cradle of the Confederacy*. New York: The New Press, 2018.

Larson, Kate Clifford. *Bound for the Promised Land: Harriet Tubman: Portrait of an American Hero*. New York: One World, 2004.

Letter from Clara Barton to "Aimee." Clara Barton National Historic Site, CLBA4490. National Park Service, Washington, DC.

Manigault-Bryant, LeRhonda S. *Talking to the Dead: Religion, Music, and Lived Memory among Gullah/Geechee Women*. Durham, NC: Duke University Press, 2014.

Military, Compiled Service Record. [Civil War]. Christopher Sancho. U.S.C.T. 21. D167.P.97.73–2200. 83–195.129. National Archives, Washington, DC.

Mille, Katherine Wyly, and Michael B. Montgomery. "Introduction." In Lorenzo Dow Turner, *Africanisms in the Gullah Dialect*. Columbia: University of South Carolina Press, 2002.

Mitchell, Faith. *Hoodoo Medicine: Gullah Herbal Remedies*. Rev. ed. Columbia, SC: Summerhouse Press, 1999.

Morgan, Philip D. *Slave Counterpoint: Black Culture in the Eighteenth-Century Chesapeake and Lowcountry*. Chapel Hill: Omohundro Institute and University of North Carolina Press, 1998.

Motsinger, Carol, and Daniel J. Gross. "His Ancestors Fought for Their Freedom in the Civil War. Now, He Fights to Preserve What They left Him." *Greenville News*, July 20, 2021.

National Park Service. *Low Country Gullah Culture Special Resource Study and Final Environmental Impact Statement.* Atlanta, GA: National Park Service, Southeast Regional Office, July 2005. https://www.nps.gov/ethnography /research/docs/ggsrs_book.pdf.

"Newspaper Account of a Meeting between Black Religious Leaders and Union Military Authorities," February 13, 1865. Freedom and Southern Society Project. University of Maryland. https://freedmen.umd.edu/savmtg.htm.

Note from Assistant General of War Department to the Commissioner of Pensions, Jan 4, 1882. Pension File. No. 933856.

Ochiai, Akiko. "The Port Royal Experiment Revisited: Northern Visions of Reconstruction and the Land Question." *The New England Quarterly* 74, no. 1 (2001): 94–117. https://doi.org/10.2307/3185461.

Opala, Joseph A. *The Gullah: Rice, Slavery, and the Sierra Leone-American Connection*. Washington, DC: United States Information Service, 1987.

Patterson, Orlando. *Slavery and Social Death: A Comparative Study, With a New Preface*. 2nd ed. Cambridge, MA: Harvard University Press, 2018.

Roberts, Blain, and Ethan J. Kytle. "When Freedom Came to Charleston." *New York Times*, February 19, 2015. https://archive.nytimes.com /opinionator.blogs.nytimes.com/2015/02/19/.

Rodney, Walter. *A History of the Upper Guinea Coast, 1545–1800*. New York: Monthly Review Press, 1970.

Schuessler, Jennifer. "Smallpox Took a Huge Toll on Emancipated Slaves, Historian Writes." *Seattle Times*, June 16, 2012.

Severson, Kim, "Finding a Lost Strain of Rice and Clues to Slave Cooking," *New York Times*, February 13, 2018. https://www.nytimes.com/2018/02/13 /dining/hill-rice-slave-history.html.

Shapiro, Michael. "Rehearsal for Reconstruction." *New York Times*, November 6, 2011.

Skinner, David E. "Mande Settlement and the Development of Islamic Institutions in Sierra Leone." *The International Journal of African Historical Studies* 11, no. 1 (1978): 32–62.

Slave Narratives. A Folk History of Slavery in the United States. Interviews with Former Slaves. Federal Writers' Project. 1936–38. Library of Congress, Washington, DC. https://www.loc.gov/item/mesn143/.

Smith, Tracy K. *To Free the Captives: A Plea for the American Soul*. New York: Knopf, 2023.

Smith, W. Calvin. "Habersham Family." *New Georgia Encyclopedia*, last modified Sept. 11, 2014. https://www.georgiaencyclopedia.org/articles/history -archaeology/habersham-family/.

Trinkley, Michael, ed. *An Archaeological Survey of the Barker Field Expansion Project, Hilton Head Island, Beaufort County, South Carolina*. Research Series 17. Columbia, SC: Chicora Foundation, August 1989.

Trinkley, Michael. *Indian and Freedman Occupation at the Fish Haul Site*. Research Series 7. Columbia, SC: Chicora Foundation, 2020. https:// dc.statelibrary.sc.gov/items.

Turner, Lorenzo Dow. *Africanisms in the Gullah Dialect*. Introduction by Katherine Wyly Mille and Michael B. Montgomery. Columbia: University of South Carolina Press, 2002. (First published in 1949)

Twitty, Michael W. *The Cooking Gene: A Journey Through African American Culinary History in the Old South*. Illustrated edition. New York: Amistad, 2017.

US Freedman's Bank Records. 1865–1874, Ancestry.com. https://www.ancestry .com/search/collections/8755/.

Index

Page numbers in italic refer to illustrations.